WEARING THE BLUE

By

Chuck Nelson

DEDICATED TO: JUSTICE AND THE JUSTIFIER

LifeRich Publishing is a registered trademark of The Reader's Digest Association, Inc.

LifeRich Publishing books may be ordered through booksellers or by contacting:

LifeRich Publishing
1663 Liberty Drive
Bloomington, IN 47403
www.liferichpublishing.com
844-686-9607

Scripture taken from the King James Version of the Bible.

ISBN: 978-1-4897-3539-3 (sc)
ISBN: 978-1-4897-3540-9 (e)

Library of Congress Control Number: 2021908432

Print information available on the last page.

LifeRich Publishing rev. date: 04/23/2021

A special thank you to Joan Olsson for her review and editing of all my books. She is able to find all the little spelling, typo, punctuation and miscellaneous errors that are invisible to me until she points them out.

CONTENTS

INTRODUCTION

Everyone has seen a police officer from the outside – the badge, gun belt, uniform, short haircut and hopefully well-shined shoes. Have you ever looked past the uniform or wondered what it's like on the inside of that uniform? How does it feel from the inside out - wearing the blue? What kind of person becomes a police officer and what kind of person does a police officer become?

In this book I will be providing an inside perspective on "wearing the blue." In the process I may be able to answer some questions you have but were hesitant to ask a man or woman wearing a gun. I hung up my gun and badge (retired) in the year 2000 so I am free to share the good, bad and ugly as you track with me in a 34 year venture from rookie to lieutenant to old salt. Obviously, every man or woman wearing the blue is different and I don't pretend to represent or speak for everyone in uniform. I can only tell you what I know and saw and how it felt from the inside out. I will try not to get too serious in the telling and will grease some of the rough spots with a bit of humor where I can. A sense of humor should be standard issue for police officers. For reasons that should become obvious as you read on, I consider a sense of humor to be almost as important as a bullet-proof vest when it comes to protecting the heart.

I already mentioned that everyone in law enforcement is different. I may be a bit more different than others in the profession because of my background. I never intended to become a cop. I loved country living and felt fortunate to have grown up on a ranch, but I knew ranching was not for me. For details on this you will have to read, *Life at The End of a Dirt Road,* my story about growing up on the ranch.

Given that becoming a police officer wasn't the culmination of a life-long dream and given that milking cows, chasing chickens and kicking cow pies doesn't really prepare one for a career in municipal law enforcement, I felt uniquely unqualified for my chosen career path. Unlike most city kids, I never had a close encounter with a police officer until I was one. When I first put on the blue and hit the streets of Oakland, California, I was almost completely unprepared for the world that confronted me. It was soon evident that I was sure as heck not in Kansas anymore.

In the pages that follow I will let you look over my shoulder as I entered into my career in law enforcement. I will share some of my thoughts and experiences as I followed this unique career path. Many of the experiences are outside the norm for most people so my thoughts and opinions may fall outside the norm as well. Read on....you have been warned.

CHAPTER 1

WHAT DO I WANT TO BE WHEN I GROW UP?

What do you want to be when you grow up? When this question was first posed to me, I was five or six years old growing up on a cattle ranch at the end of a dirt road in Siskiyou County, California. At this age, I decided to become a cowboy. The decision was, no doubt, influenced by the horses, cattle, and trappings of the ranch around me. My folks seemed to approve of this career path and often encouraged me to tell other adults who would visit the ranch from time to time. They also smiled and approved so my career path seemed set. I figured a cowboy's job was to wear a cowboy outfit and mosey around on a horse and that sounded pretty good to me at the time.

By the time I was well into elementary school I had matured and abandoned the idea of growing up to be a cowboy. As I looked around, I noticed there weren't any cowboys except in the movies. (This was long before we had TV.) I decided I was around 100 years too late for a proper cowboy career. This wasn't a problem because I loved to draw pictures and decided I wanted to be a cartoonist when I grew up.

In high school, I took art classes and found that while I might be a little better than average at art, I was nowhere near skilled enough to be a cartoonist. I realized I would probably get pretty hungry trying to make a living on my art. The "what do you want to be when you grow up" question haunted me as my high school years drew to a close. The question had come to me in various forms through the years but now I was beginning to realize that I would soon have to provide an answer for those who ask but, more importantly, for myself. By this time, I had ruled out jet pilot, cowboy and cartoonist but what line of work or career did I want to dedicate my life to? As high school came to an end, I had no definitive answer for others or myself. I thought, perhaps I'll figure it out in college.

When I arrived in Sacramento California to attend Sacramento State College, I was an out of place naïve country kid. I had grown up on a cattle ranch in far northern California and attended small town schools. Life in the big city was uncomfortable and foreign to me and I was sure that anybody who saw me would immediately recognize me as a hick from the sticks.

In my senior year of high school, I had received a letter from the gymnastics coach at Sacramento State College inviting me to attend college at Sac State where I could participate on the gymnastic team. The coach, Irv Faria, had seen me perform at Yreka High School when on a recruiting tour disguised as a gymnastic clinic and, on that basis, sent the invitation. It was just an invitation, nothing like a scholarship but it was the tipping point in my struggle to decide which college to attend. I had no idea what I would major in, but college seemed to be a good place to be until I figured out who I was supposed to be. I found comfort in the discovery that many other freshmen college entrants were as clueless as I was about their future.

In September of 1962 I arrived on campus too late to get a room in the dorm, so I ended up in an off campus boarding house with several other young men. The boarding house was several miles from campus, so I took a bus to campus each day. Before long, the bus trips to campus, classes, and gymnastics workouts became a comfortable routine. While still uncomfortable with city life I found I could tolerate it.

In college, nobody asks you, "What do you want to be when you grow up?" They ask the same question in another way, "What's your major?" The first two years of college were pretty much filled with required courses, so I still had time to figure out who I was supposed to be when I grew up. It seems that young people in college are always asking others, "What's your major?" When I asked one of the guys in the boarding house what his major was, he said, "police science." I had never heard of such a major, so I asked him what it was all about, and he said that it was very interesting, and he studied law, criminal procedure, evidence, search and seizure, and such.

I had never in all my life to this point considered going into law enforcement but the courses he was talking about sounded interesting. I looked in the school course catalog and found the major was called "public administration with a specialization in general police administration." The course descriptions were very interesting, so I decided to take an exploratory course in the subject area. I took a course called "criminal law" that was being taught by Earl Warren Jr. I was vaguely aware that the instructor's father had been governor of California and Chief Justice of the Supreme Court, but this didn't impress or distract me as my primary interest was in the course. It turned out that Earl Warren Jr. was an excellent instructor and his interest in law was contagious....at least it was for me. At the end of the course, I wanted more so I declared my major as "public administration with a specialization in general police administration." I loved the courses I was taking and finally thought I had some sort of an idea of what I wanted to be when I grew up. I didn't know exactly what line of law enforcement I would end up in. Would I be in municipal law enforcement, a rural sheriff department, or something in state or federal law enforcement? I had no idea where it would lead but I liked the direction I was headed.

I eventually managed to get into the men's dormitory on campus and this reduced my commute from a bus to a walk. I think today the dorms are all co-ed but back then there were separate dormitories for males and females. I wonder if this new co-ed arrangement could possibly lead to complications or problems in dorm life?

In my final two years of college my major required me to take an internship job in law enforcement. I landed a part time job with the California Division of Forestry or CDF in their Law Enforcement Division. Today it's called Cal Fire but in that day, it was CDF. I was very fortunate to end up with a great boss, Lou Gerlinger, who took me under his wing and was a great mentor. He teased me endlessly for my Christian faith, but I took it as just kidding and let it go.

I worked in a small office high in the Resources Building in downtown Sacramento. Wow! Look at me...one day I'm a kid milking cows in the sticks and now I'm a city boy working on the 15th floor in an office building in downtown Sacramento….with a window no less. I'm not sure of all the state offices in the building but Fish and Game had offices there as well as the CDF.

While working with the CDF I provided the various field law enforcement personnel with mug shots and rap sheets of arson releases to their district. In case you are out of the loop on this, when someone convicted of arson is released from prison the state notifies certain agencies in the jurisdiction where the arsonist will reside, and the CDF was routinely notified. It was my job to order a mug shot (photograph) and rap sheet (listing of criminal arrests and convictions) from the state and provide this to the various CDF district offices where the arsonists were being released. I attended meetings and training events with my boss and, for the first time, earned peace officer status and was authorized to carry a gun. This was a big deal for me, and I felt great pride and responsibility to be entrusted with this authority.

During the summer between my junior and senior years I was able to work full time for the CDF. The campus dorms were closed so the CDF put me up in some barracks of a sort near the town of Davis. The facility was used as a place for CDF personnel to stay when traveling about the state. It was very rudimentary with a room slightly larger than a closet with a bed. They even had a cook on staff to cook breakfast for us before we went off to work. The cook was a lady that I estimated to be between 150 and 200 years old, very cranky, and likely had poor eyesight as she put pepper on the eggs she undercooked until she could see it. By the time she could see the pepper on the eggs they were approaching black. It was hard for anybody else to see the egg beneath the pepper; however, she entertained no complaints. I was thankful to have a place to sleep, such as it was, and breakfast, such as it was, so I was in no position to complain.

While in college and working for the CDF I became engaged to Valerie Grey, the wonderful girl who would become my wife. Before our marriage I had taken a test for a state investigator job and on September 3rd of 1965 my CDF boss came to me with a newspaper clipping where the City of Oakland was looking for "policemen" applicants. In that day Oakland had policeman positions and policewoman positions but today they are all called "police officers" because both male and female applicants are sought. My boss told me that the Oakland Police Department has a great reputation as a progressive police department, and I might want to look into it. I did a little research and found OPD had a good reputation and was considered modern in every way. The starting salary was $663 a month which was a great salary in that day.

I had visited grandparents who lived in Oakland during my youth and felt a connection with the city, so I requested an application. After returning the completed application, I was given a date for a two-hour written examination on September 28, 1965. I passed the written exam and was scheduled for a physical agility and oral interview on September 30th. Shortly before Val and I were married on April 2nd, 1966, I received notice for a psychiatric evaluation on April 6th and a medical examination on April 7th. Val and I were married on the 2nd and I attended these evaluations while on our honeymoon in San Francisco. After our marriage I moved into Val's apartment in Sacramento for the duration of my senior year at college. At about this time I was notified that I had passed the state investigator job and was offered a position, but I passed on it as I was hoping for the job with more potential at OPD.

On April 14th, I received a phone call from a Lieutenant Lewis of OPD informing me that I had passed all tests and should report for work, which would begin with a police academy, on June 13th. I was excited beyond words but also apprehensive. Things were happening fast, a marriage, an exciting job offer, graduation from college, a pending move to a new city. My, or I should say, "our" heads were spinning.

Val and I made a trip to Oakland and secured an apartment. I also had to purchase certain required uniform and equipment items which I needed to have before entering the police academy. I graduated from Sacramento State College on June 10th, a Friday and on the next day we moved into our Oakland apartment on McClure Street. The following Monday, June 13th, 1966 I reported to work at the OPD, joining into the second week of the eight week academy which was called the "43 Basic School."

I should point out that my decision to go into law enforcement was based on more than the fact that I found the academic course more interesting than anything else I looked at in the college curriculum manual. I was suffering from the naïve idea that people in law enforcement were, for the most part, or certainly should be, the good guys. My decision for this career path was made during the years when there were race riots in places like Los Angeles and Cleveland. My perspective on these matters was obtained from newspapers and TV reports which pointed to racism and police misconduct and injustice as contributing causes. My naïve thinking was that if I went into law enforcement, I could make a difference. I could set an example of unbiased conduct. I would show how all people could be treated fairly in the justice system and I could demonstrate that not all police officers were prejudiced.

I thought I would be different, I would stand out as an example of truth, justice and the American way. I would be catching bad guys and protecting good guys. What could go wrong? I was pathetically naïve and idealistic. My motives weren't wrong, but I lacked understanding and real-world perspective. In my defense I would say I probably wasn't much different from many young people just out of college and facing the world on their own. At that age, armed with idealism and insulated by ignorance, we are ready to change the world.

I was completely unaware of the danger I was approaching. Not the physical danger so much as the psychological danger. I was an idealist. An idealist is vulnerable in the real world. I once read that a cynic is an idealist turned inside out. Wow! Did I find this to be true! When an idealist runs into the brick wall of the real world there is the real danger of being turned inside out. I was unaware of this until I saw it happening around me on the job. During much of my career in law enforcement I struggled to temper idealism with reality to avoid the collision that turned others to cynics. I think it's a good thing for someone to enter law enforcement with positive idealistic intentions. However, the balance between idealism and realism is a delicate and seemingly constant struggle in this line of work. It was for me much of the time, especially during my early years in my career.

I was a relatively new Christian at the time I entered law enforcement. My faith and Christian perspective gave me an advantage in my law enforcement career. As I matured in my faith and Christian perspective, it became easier to cope with the reality of the street. The fresh out of college idealist who was going to change the world would find that the biggest battle was not crime and dealing with the rough edge of society. The biggest battle was to not to let the world change me into something I didn't want to be.

CHAPTER 2

THE POLICE ACADEMY

Early in the morning on June 13th, 1966 I found myself in downtown Oakland walking along 7th street toward the Oakland Police Administration building (PAB) at 7th and Broadway. It was my first day of work with the Oakland Police Department and I had no idea what to expect. There were just four years of college between me and life on a remote cattle ranch. Now I was going to be a big city cop. I was excited, determined and petrified at the same time.

It was an overcast and cool morning and on the outside I would have appeared confident but on the inside, I felt like a hay seed blowing along the streets of Oakland. Who was I to be an Oakland Police Officer? What lay ahead of me; would I be able to deal with the physical and emotional demands of police work? Motivated by idealism and insulated by naivety I was determined to succeed.

My first "assignment" with the Oakland Police department was the police academy. While it was what people would refer to generically as a police academy it was officially known as the 43rd Basic Recruit School. I was one of 17 recruit officers in the class. Fourteen of the recruits were Oakland police officers, one was an Oakland Park ranger, one was with the City of Walnut Creek and another with the City of Alameda. Together we were Oakland's 43rd Basic Recruit School.

A police academy or recruit school is the typical starting place for a career in municipal law enforcement. The academy is an intense course of physical and academic training that is designed to prepare recruits for the job ahead. Much of the training is required by the California Commission on Police Officers Standards and Training (POST). POST sets the minimum selection and training standards for California law enforcement and law enforcement agencies or college courses seeking POST certification must comply with those standards. Graduates from a POST certified academy are awarded a Basic POST certificate.

It's very time consuming and expensive to put on a police academy so it's common for smaller agencies to send their personnel to a larger agency's academy or require new hires to come with a Basic POST certificate acquired from an accredited training program. The time and expense of POST training encourages the concept of regional academies where resources can be pooled. Still, larger agencies prefer to put on their own academies because they can ensure quality control and incorporate training in their own rules, regulations, procedures and philosophy as well as any local municipal or county laws and ordinances.

Years later, a Basic POST certified course required 599 hours of instruction in 42 different domains or areas of instruction that include such things as first aid, criminal law, laws of arrest and evidence and domestic violence. On top of this, POST required another 65 hours of testing bringing the Basic Academy time requirement up to 664 hours. This stretched the academy to something over 16 weeks even before an agency interjects its own rules, procedures, policies, and local laws. I'm sure the POST requirements have continued to evolve since my retirement.

By contrast, the OPD academy I attended in 1966 was eight weeks long – and I only attended seven of the eight weeks. Because the academy started the week before I graduated from college, I entered the academy a week late and had to borrow other student's notes to study so I could take tests on the subject matters covered on the first week that I missed. I managed to catch up and came in second in class standing at the end of the academy. Another college graduate, somewhat uncommon in those days, came in just ahead of me as valedictorian.

By the end of my career at OPD, the length of police academies had doubled since 1966 primarily because more domains have been added to the basic POST requirements and the amount of instruction time in other areas had been increased. I would say that, for the most part, the increase in instruction is justified. Law enforcement is a complex discipline involving ever changing procedures, regulations, and laws of arrest, search and seizure. Technology evolves also and new technologies, however helpful and welcomed, add complexity to the job. For better or for worse, cultural conditions, roles and expectations change also and law enforcement personnel must be tuned to the current frequency if they are to be in tune with the modern culture. A significant amount of training is necessary before you give a man or woman a gun and turn them loose on the public with the instruction to "go out and catch bad guys."

I would have to admit that there's some fluff in the Basic POST training requirements. Sometimes a domain is assigned a specific amount of training time based more on its perceived social importance than the complexity of the subject matter. Like so many things in our culture, police training can sometimes be driven by the winds of political correctness. I recall the complaints of some trainers who were assigned to teach a course with no more than two hours of material which they were required to "cram" into four hours of classroom instruction because that was the amount of time POST required.

In spite of the fluff, POST certified training for California law enforcement personnel is some of the best in the nation. The longer training academies today are, for the most part, well justified and help ensure a better trained and more professional officer on the street. Unfortunately, it wasn't always like this. POST was established by the California State Legislature in 1959. Prior to this, much of the training for law enforcement personnel was hit and miss and dependent on the professionalism of the particular agency.

When I first came on the Oakland Police Department, I was told by some of the old timers that they were given a badge and a gun on their first day of work and told to get out there and catch bad guys and direct traffic. There was little or no formal training. This reminds me of a saying that holds that good judgment comes from experience, but experience comes from bad judgment. Today, turning untrained officers onto the street to learn primarily by trial and error is, thankfully, a thing of the past. It's not that modern "trained" officers don't make mistakes; it's just that good training can help officers avoid many mistakes because much of good training is built on the mistakes of generations of police officers before us. Thanks to modern training it's no longer necessary to make mistakes to learn from them and it's even better when knowledge, conduct and procedures learned from training equip officers to anticipate and avoid problems and mistakes in the first place.

As indicated earlier, I entered the Oakland Police academy with a great deal of apprehension. Prior to arriving at the academy, I had received detailed instructions on what to wear, how to cut my hair and how to conduct myself in the academy. Our academy uniform consisted of a particular brand of green work clothes that had to be heavily starched and pressed with military creases. I had no idea what a military crease was but, fortunately, I found a laundry that knew what I needed. I was not used to such regimentation and found it a bit intimidating.

The police academy was my first encounter with the paramilitary environment common to many law enforcement agencies. One of the first things we learned was to refer to personnel of higher rank by their rank rather than their first name. This was fine with me as I found it much easier to refer to people by the title "sergeant" or "lieutenant" than to try to remember everybody's name. As a rookie I quickly learned I could get along well just by referring to everybody else as "sir."

On my first day in the academy, I was issued several pounds worth of manuals. Like most departments, Oakland had a General Order Manual. Our General Order Manual was about five inches thick and filled with rules and procedures instructing us on everything from how to make photocopies to when to use your firearm. Each order was signed "By order of"…the chief of police and constituted standing orders that required compliance.

A second manual we were issued was called Rules and Regulations and, as the name implies it was full of rules of conduct and regulations for such things as uniforms and equipment. It was only about an inch thick but still chocked full of dos and don'ts.

Then there was a Report Writing Manual. It was a couple inches thick and provided instruction on how to properly complete various types of forms and reports and which reports to complete under which circumstances.

Finally, there was a series of Training Manuals that ranged from one to three inches thick. They provided training tips, legal information and/

or more procedures, rules, and regulations for various types of police incidents.

This mound of manuals was as intimidating as it was overwhelming. How could anyone ever get a handle on the information, rules, regulations, threats and suggestions contained in all these manuals? It seemed that it would be almost impossible to get through a day without inadvertently violating a do or don't somewhere in one of those manuals. Every time a new rule, regulation, order or training bulletin was added, deleted or modified, we were required (supposed) to remove the old one and insert the new one in the appropriate manual and update the index accordingly. I was very conscientious in this for most of my career.

Starting with the police academy and throughout my law enforcement career, I found it useful to reduce the important elements of critical orders and rules and manuals onto 3 X 5 cards which I could study and carry with me as necessary. This habit became even more useful later in my career when I studied for promotional advancement.

Because I had just come through college finals, the academic requirements of the academy were not that difficult. All it took was some study discipline to keep on top of things. We were required to type our classroom notes and present them for inspection periodically. I have always been a note taker, so this involved a lot of typing but it was a useful part of the learning process. In that day a word processor consisted of a brain and a typewriter. Once again, I was thankful that I took a typing class in high school. A PC with word processing would have made my note typing much easier but such equipment wasn't around for us in 1966.

Class began each day with physical inspection where we were lined up at attention in a hallway while a training officer, sergeant or lieutenant or someone of appropriate authority inspected us. The inspections were formal, and we were given commands in semi-military fashion. First, we were told to "fall in." With this command we all formed a single line while facing forward. The next order was "at close interval, dress right dress." Upon this command we each turned our head to the left and extended our left arm with fingers together and extended to touch the right shoulder of the person to our left. We quickly shuffled our feet to space ourselves to a perfect arm's length. The next command was "ready front." On this command we came to attention with our arms to the side and faces forward while we were inspected.

This was all new to me and I thought it was cool. I had not been in the military and it seemed orderly and efficient. Little did I know that when assigned to Patrol Division for the rest of my career at Oakland I would either be inspected in this manner or I would inspect others in this manner at *lineup* before going onto the street.

In the academy the inspections were rather strict, and we soon learned that our belt buckle was supposed to line up with our fly and shirt buttons. Our uniform needed to be clean and pressed each day. Our shoes needed to be spit-shined and we had better have a proper haircut. We were told to show up with a military haircut and I had been to the barber and asked for a military haircut. However, upon my first inspection I was told to get a haircut so, after class, off I went for another "military" haircut which was a notch more than a shaved head. On my first inspection I was also told to shine my shoes. I had spent a lot of time shining my shoes, but I had never seen a spit-shine until I saw everyone else's shoes at lineup. I got detailed instruction from fellow recruits on how to spit-shine my shoes and, after my haircut, study, and typing my notes I spit-shined my shoes and leather gear.

After a few weeks we were sometimes required to report for our morning inspection in our regular police uniform and leather gear with weapon. It felt good to wear a proper police uniform rather than our green rookie outfit. The green outfit was essentially work clothes with a military press. Our police uniform would have to be properly pressed and all leather gear spit shined. Sometimes the inspection would be in short sleeve uniform shirt, sometimes in long sleeve uniform shirt and sometimes in dress uniform with long sleeve shirt, tie, white gloves, and tunic. Always with our police cap on.

I confess that it felt good to be all shined up and standing at attention in dress uniform. I felt a pride welling up inside me that seemed like it was going to burst out of my chest. I had acquired my uniform and leather gear prior to reporting to the academy and you can be assured that I put some of it on and checked myself out in front of a mirror. As I posed in front of a mirror, I decided I looked rather cool. I was no longer the awkward kid who milked cows on the ranch.

The academy was always a bit tense for a number of reasons. First, everything was new to me. I was going through this experience with a number of other people who were also experiencing it for the first time and there was a bond of camaraderie in that. However, I was outranked by everybody above the rank of "officer" and, as a recruit I was technically not an "officer." Everybody but the janitor outranked me and even the civilian employees of the police department knew more than I did.

In addition to academic training on criminal law, police procedures, departmental rules and regulations, we had physical training, defensive tactics and firearms training. Firearms training included instruction on how to clean your weapon and we had to present our gun for inspection on the following morning's daily inspection. I had grown up around guns and hunting so handling firearms wasn't new to me. Still, I learned new skills and acquired a level of competence and confidence I didn't have previously.

On July 29th, 1966, I graduated from the Oakland Police Department's 43rd Basic School. I was one of 14 Oakland Police Officers in the academy. There was also one Alameda and one Walnut Creek officer as well as an Oakland Park Ranger in attendance. In the years that followed, one of us would be killed in the line of duty and most of the attendees would leave the department for one reason or another before retiring.

By the time I graduated from the Oakland Police recruit academy, between college and the academy, I had received hundreds of hours of training in law and procedure and various related law enforcement subjects. Still, in the back of my mind, I was wondering how I would do on the street, in the real world. How does book-learning work on the street? The street is where, in the heat of the moment, I would have to weigh actions, observations and statements against academic concepts of law, procedure and evidence to make real time decisions pertaining to detention, arrest, and use of force. It didn't escape my mind that these would potentially be life and death decisions for myself or others. These are not realities that one should take lightly....and I didn't.

CHAPTER 3

THE ROOKIE GOES
TO LINEUP

Near the end of the police academy, we each received a copy of a Personnel Order from the office of the Chief of Police. Personnel Orders come out periodically reflecting additions, terminations, promotions, and transfers of personnel within the department. This particular order reflected the fact that all OPD officers in the academy and assigned to the Training Section were to be transferred to the Patrol Division on the day after the academy ended. We were each assigned to one of the three shifts or watches. I discovered that I was assigned to third watch, also called the swing shift.

To help the reader understand the terms and organization of the Department, I will define some terms and give a brief simplified description of the departmental organization:

If you were looking at an organizational chart of the Department in that day, you would see three bureaus under the Chief of Police. Each bureau was headed by a deputy chief of police. The three bureaus were the BUREAU OF SERVICES, the BUREAU OF INVESTIGATION and the BUREAU OF FIELD OPERATIONS.

The BUREAU OF SERVICES consisted of units like the Records Division, Jail Division, Communications Division, Personnel and Training Division and Planning Division.

The BUREAU OF INVESTIGATION consisted of units like the Criminal Investigation Division (CID), Criminalistics Section, Internal Affairs Section, Vice Control Division and Youth Services Division.

The BUREAU OF FIELD OPERATIONS consisted of the Patrol Division, Traffic Division and Animal Control Section.

In simplified terms, the PATROL DIVISION was divided into three shifts which we called watches. If you think of a work shift as 8 hours, you don't have to be a great mathematician to see that three 8-hour shifts will cover a 24-hour day. The first watch (also called dogwatch) was the first shift of the day and went from 12 midnight to 8:00 AM. The second watch (called day shift) went from 8:00 AM to 4:00 PM and the third watch (called swing shift) went from 4:00 PM to 12:00 AM. In reality, personnel assigned to a watch were divided into two groups with one group arriving one hour earlier than the other so that at shift change we didn't pull everybody off the street at once.

With this background you can now understand that when I was assigned to the third watch, I would be working from 4:00 PM to 12:00 AM. If assigned to the earlier shift, I would work from 3:00 PM to 11:00 PM. Not to complicate things too much, I should point out that we actually worked an eight and a half hour shift. For instance, if we were assigned to the 8:00 AM to 4:00 PM shift we were technically on duty until 4:30 PM while our relief personnel were attending *lineup* which was when personnel were inspected, briefed and given their assignments. If all of this is too complicated, just think of personnel being assigned to one of three shifts which we called watches. First watch was midnights, second watch was day shift, and third watch was swing shift.

I'll describe personnel assigned to each watch and how we were deployed over the city. In the process, I'll define some terms that you may find helpful as you read on. Each watch had a watch commander who was a captain of police. For purposes of deployment, the city was divided into geographic areas called BEATS. Normally, at least one police officer was assigned to each beat. The beat sizes varied because they were originally created to account for roughly the same number of calls for service. Busy beats with lots of calls for service were smaller and larger beats were where there were fewer calls for service. When my career started, the city was divided into 29 beats.

Adjacent beats were organized into what we called DISTRICTS. A sergeant of police was assigned to a district and responsible for supervision of personnel assigned to that district. In that day, the City of Oakland was divided into 29 beats which were divided into 5 districts.

In addition to beats and districts, there was one more division. For police purposes, the city was divided into two SECTORS. Sector 1 consisted of Districts 1 and 2 and covered West and North Oakland. Sector two consisted of districts 3,4 and 5 which was East Oakland. A Lieutenant of police was assigned to supervise personnel and activities in a sector.

If you are following me, each watch had a captain who was the watch commander, two lieutenants who were sector commanders, and five sergeants who were district supervisors. After this, various officers were assigned to beats. Actually, there were more sergeants and officers assigned to a watch than there were beats and districts as there were floating relief teams that filled in during the days off of personnel normally assigned to a particular District. Each watch was self-contained to staff all positions seven days a week.

In addition to officers assigned to beats, each watch had officers trained and assigned to be evidence technicians to process crime scenes and some officers were assigned to drive prisoner transport vehicles which we called paddy wagons or just wagons. Having prisoner transport vehicles on hand helped keep the beat officer on the job in the field rather than tying him/her up transporting an arrestee to jail. While beats were originally designed to have roughly the same volume of calls for service or work load, demographics change, and some beats exceed the ability of a single assigned officer, so some beats had two officers assigned. For instance, there were two officers normally assigned to downtown beat 2, one would be 2A and one would be 2B.

In addition to chain of command issues, the division of the City into two sectors made a logical division for assigned radio channels. Under normal conditions one radio channel was assigned to sector 1 for dispatching calls for service to field personnel and another channel was assigned to sector two. The City of Oakland is a busy city with too much police radio traffic to be handled on a single assigned channel most of the time. If you are a beat officer in trouble and waiting for a break in the

18

radio traffic so you can call for help you can understand why heavy radio traffic is problematic. Lake Merritt served as a logical physical boundary between sector 1 and 2 and their assigned radio channels.

I've described the various personnel, geographic and logistic considerations to give you a background and perspective one might have on the first day on the job. In addition to all the book learning you got in college and the academy, you now have to figure out how to find the beat you are assigned to, the correct radio channel to use, the boundaries of your assigned beat, how to find any location quickly on your beat or any other beat, the correct radio codes to use, and much more.

So, there I was, a rookie fresh out of recruit school (the academy) assigned to the third watch. This is a test...what were my working hours? If you passed the test, you know I was assigned to work from 3:00 PM to 11:30PM or from 4:00 PM to 12:30 AM. The odd numbered beats reported to the early lineup and even numbered beats reported to the late lineup. On the outside, I looked like everyone else but on the inside, there was nervous anticipation. The rubber was about to meet the road. I admit, I didn't quite look exactly like everyone else on the watch, my shiny leather and fresh uniform distinguished me as a rookie. Most of the officers had a bit of shine on their shoes and leather gear but not the spit shine characteristic of the police academy. The faces as well as the gear of the old salts showed the years of wear.

To give you a feel for what it was like when officers reported for duty, I'll describe the routine we called the lineup. While there were variations in how lineup was conducted, I'll give you an idea of how it was typically done in my day. If you were assigned to work the 4:00 to 12:30 shift you were expected to be in the lineup room and in your seat at 4:00, not 4:01 PM. At the front of the room was a platform raised a step above the floor. There was a podium and the watch captain usually stood behind the podium while, a lieutenant and the sergeants sat in chairs on the platform facing out into the room. Officers sat in chairs in front of and facing the command and supervisory staff at the front of the room.

On a typical day, the captain or one of the lieutenants would tell everyone to "fall out for inspection." On this order the officers would get out of their chairs and walk out of the lineup room into a hallway. This would usually be accompanied by some grumbling under their breath. The officers would form a line with toes on the edge of the floor tiles in the middle of the hallway. Just as we had experienced it in the academy, the captain would order in a loud voice, "At close interval dress right (pause) dress." With this command, officers would remain facing forward but turn their head to their left and extend their left arm to touch the right shoulder of the officer to their left. There would be some shuffling of feet as everyone established their spacing. When everyone was properly spaced, the captain would say, "Ready (pause) front." With this command, officers would drop their arms to their side and turn their head to face forward standing more or less at attention.

Next, the captain or perhaps the lieutenant would move down the line in front of and then behind the officers inspecting each one. Was their uniform clean and without tears or obvious repairs, was their badge on and clean, was their cap and cap badge clean, were there any buttons undone, did everyone have all their gear on and in good order. Sometimes the inspecting command officer would have a sergeant follow him with a clipboard during the inspection to make note of any discrepancies to be followed up on.

On occasion during inspection the command officer would announce a weapons inspection and order everyone to, "about face, unload and holster your weapon." Everyone would follow that direction and return to facing front. The command to "present arms" was given, and officers would draw their weapon and hold it upward at a 45-degree angle with their elbow at their side. The inspecting command officer would walk down the line taking possession of each weapon in turn and check it for cleanliness and function.

At the end of the inspection, the command officer would order "fall out" and everyone would return to the lineup room and take a seat for roll call. The captain or whoever he designated would then call roll and make assignments. Prior to lineup, one of the lieutenants would prepare a duty roster which assigned personnel to their beat or other assignment for the shift. The roll call and duty assignment during lineup would go something like this; the captain would say, "Nelson" the officer would respond, "Here sir" and the captain would say, "You're working beat 14." "Smith." "here sir," "You're working beat 22." "Johnson," "here sir" "Blanchard," "here sir" "you are working 41 wagon." The wagon assignment was a prisoner transport vehicle that looked something like a bread truck with police markings, but it was always a two-officer assignment.

While the captain was taking roll call and announcing assignments, the sergeants would be busy walking among the officers and handing out subpoenas, warrants to be served on their beat assignment and any correspondence directed to individual officers.

After roll call and assignments, the captain or an assigned lieutenant would brief officers on any major incidents from the previous shift and report on relevant departmental changes or issues. It was common to discuss and remind officers of any relevant training, safety and procedural matters during lineup.

Every day a listing of stolen vehicles, which we called a hot sheet, was made available to all officers going on duty. A *hot sheet* usually filled the better part of an 8x11 sheet of paper. This enabled officers to check suspicious vehicles for stolen status and especially when making a car stop. In addition, a *daily bulletin* was provided to each officer. The daily bulletin included listings of alerts, wants and cautions as well as relevant departmental announcements. The marked cars that officers drove were called *beat cars* and they had a clipboard mounted for easy access by the driver. The daily bulletin was usually placed on the clipboard for easy reference during the tour of duty and the hot sheet was mounted on top for easy quick reference at a glance.

When lineup was concluded, the command officer would announce, "dismissed," or "be safe out there," or "make relief." This was the order to go to work. The expression to "make relief" was used because there was a shift of personnel waiting to go off duty when relieved of duty by the oncoming shift.

In the early part of my career, almost all cars assigned to field duty were one-man cars. It was unusual to have two officers assigned to a car. A few years into my career it was more common to have two people assigned to a car for safety reasons.

It is interesting to note that when I first went onto the Oakland Police department, the job title for officers was called "Patrolman." At that time, all uniformed personnel working the street were men. There was a job titled "Police Woman" but they were few and not ordinarily assigned to uniformed street duty. Interestingly, at this same time all police dispatchers, the people who answered telephone calls for service and dispatched police officers on the police radio were male. In subsequent years, females were hired as officers and dispatchers and the job title for officers was changed from patrolman to the gender-neutral term police officer.

I have described what the police lineup was like so you can imagine how I experienced it for the first time as a fresh-out-of-recruit-school rookie. It had something of a semi-military feel but there was also some humor exchanged. While it was all new and unique to me it didn't feel repressive. It felt organized and serious. I felt a combination of pride and apprehension. I had come through a fairly intense selection and training process but now I was about to go onto the streets of Oakland where there would be dangers and challenges that I had never experienced before. I was determined but my confidence was a bit wobbly.

When my name was called for the first time in my first lineup, it went something like this. "Long," "here sir." "long you're on beat 29." "Nelson," that's me so I said, "here sir" trying to sound confident and self-assured. "Nelson, you're going to ride with Long on 29." That was it, my first assignment was a beat in far east Oakland.

When I first came on the department, there wasn't a formal training program beyond the recruit school. Later, there was a formal field training program but in my day a rookie was paired up with an experienced officer for an undetermined period of time. My field training was to ride with experienced officers in order to watch and learn from them. In retrospect, I was fortunate to have been paired with good men.

CHAPTER 4

THE ROOKIE GOES TO THE STREET

I had just attended my first lineup without seriously embarrassing myself and now I was about to undergo my very first shift as a police officer on the streets of Oakland. I would be working beat 29 with officer Long. To get to our police vehicle, we walked from the lineup room through a hallway that went under sixth street to the police Transportation facility which was located behind the police department on the south side of 6th street. The transportation facility took up an entire block and included parking for marked and unmarked police cars when not in use. The facility had a building that was normally staffed by civilian personnel who would assign vehicles to police personnel as needed. The active marked cars, the beat cars, would park along the street and the oncoming officer would normally obtain the key from the officer going off duty.

There was a small routine one did when accessing a car to begin a tour of duty. You might walk around the car to check for unusual damage, and you might check to see if your lights and siren were in order. You would put your hot sheet and daily bulletin on the clipboard and, invariably, you would open the back door and pop the back seat cushion out of place so you could look under the seat to see if there was any contraband, like weapons or drugs. The beat cars had a cage between the front and back seat and the back seat was where prisoners were placed during your tour of duty. If a prisoner is not thoroughly searched before being placed in the back of a patrol car, they will often dump a weapon or drugs under the seat. During your work shift, if you check under the seat and find contraband after removing a prisoner, you can charge them for possession of any drugs or illegal weapons because you can testify that you had previously checked and there was nothing there when you took possession of the vehicle. If we were being thorough in our inspection, we would also check the trunk.

Once our gear was stowed in the car, we were ready to roll. The gear usually included a brief case or some container which was filled with the various types of reports and forms we would need as well as extra pens and pencils and any personal gear we wanted to take with us. I always kept a street guide with me as I was unfamiliar with the streets of Oakland. When working alone, I usually brought a sack lunch which my wife (bless her heart) insisted on making for me each day. When doubled up with another officer I didn't take a lunch as we would likely eat at a restaurant or some sort of fast-food place.

It was summer when the academy concluded, and I was unfamiliar with the Bay Area weather. During the summer, the hot sun warms inland valleys causing air to rise. As the warm inland air rises, it draws clouds inland from over the cool ocean. These low clouds over Oakland are typically called fog which confused me as I had not previously heard of clouds being called fog. In any event, the cool low clouds looked like rain clouds to me. I grew up on a ranch and I could read the weather (or so I thought) so I would often take rain gear with me when I went on the street. This brought no small amount of kidding from other officers who were familiar with the Bay Area's summer "fog."

I climbed into the beat car with officer Long whose first name was Craig, and we hit the freeway to drive to beat 29 in far East Oakland. I continued to feel insecure on the inside but did my best to portray self-confidence on the outside. Craig was friendly and didn't seem to look down on me as a rookie, so I was comfortable with him.

Soon after we arrived on the beat, we got a call for service. That's what we called it when given an assignment over the police radio. The call would have gone like this, "329" that was our call sign, our identification, and it was up to beat officers to hear our call out of the background of busy radio traffic. When you are first on the street as a rookie, it takes time to learn how to listen closely to the radio traffic to know what is going on around you and recognize when you are being called. Of course, I totally missed it, but Craig heard it and responded with, "329." The dispatcher, responded with, "329, 950 on a 459 at 8275 Railroad Ave. (or whatever the address was), see Johnson the RP."

I will decode the call for the reader. All these numbers have meanings which we had memorized as part of our training, but it takes some time before everything makes sense without having to mentally translate numbers to meanings. Our call sign "329" consisted of the shift number 3 (third watch) and 29, our assigned beat. The day shift (2nd watch) call sign would have been 229 and our first watch relief would be 129.

When I first went on the streets, almost all beat cars were operated by one officer. Two person beat cars were the exception and usually consisted of a rookie and an experienced officer. When dispatched to a potentially hazardous call, two cars would be sent for safety reasons. Eventually it was determined that some beats during certain hours should have two-person beat cars for officer safety and to avoid having to send two cars. When two-person beat cars became common, the radio call signs were modified so dispatchers and field officers would know if a car was staffed by one or two officers. A one-person beat car was designated by the letter "L" and a two-person car would be designated by the letter "A." A 3rd watch car staffed by one officer assigned to beat 29 would have the call sign "3L29." A two-officer car assigned to beat 12 on the 1st watch would be called "1A12" (that might sound familiar to some who remember the TV program by that name).

So now, with this background, we could know who a dispatcher was talking to and we could tune our ear for our call sign. It takes time to get used to this. In our training we were made aware that the voice of a dispatcher carried the authority of the chief of police. A radio assignment was not an option, it was an order and failure to respond and handle the assignment was subject to discipline. We also knew that failure to respond by radio when hailed by dispatch was considered a miscall. If a dispatcher were to call "3L29" several times with no response from unit 3L29, a miscall would be declared and subject to supervisory follow-up. Typically, another unit would be dispatched to 3L29's last known location to check the wellbeing of the officer who wasn't answering his radio.

Now, let's translate what the dispatcher said on my first ever assignment as a police officer. *"329 950 on a 459 at (location), the RP is Johnson."* You already know that "329" was our shift and beat call sign. The "950" that followed was police code for "take a report." Ironically, my officer's badge number was 950 so I was destined to write many police reports in my career. The "459" was the Penal Code section for burglary. The address was where we were to go, the "RP" stood for reporting party and "Johnson" was the name of the person (reporting party) who called the police. The person calling in could be the "complainant" meaning the victim of the crime or a "reporting party" who called the police but was not necessarily the victim of the crime. In summary, my first call for service as a working police officer was to go to a particular location to see a person named Johnson who wanted to report a burglary.

This was it, I thought to myself. This is serious, we are going to investigate a burglary. We arrived at the designated location which was a small office in the corner of a junk yard which was full of junk cars and no small amount of clutter. The office was as run down and cluttered as you would expect of a junk yard office. Craig did all the talking to Mr. Johnson. I stood in the background and tried my best to look intelligent while Craig handled the report. The door to the office had been kicked in and, as I recall, some loose change and small items were missing. From my perspective, the door that had been kicked in was likely the most valuable item in the office. When Craig had all the information he needed for his report, we left a "tech tag" with Mr. Johnson and went to our car where Craig completed his report. A "tech tag" is the name of a form we completed which an evidence technician would use to coordinate his report with the report made by Craig, the reporting officer (RO). Craig notified dispatch and when available, an evidence technician would be dispatched to contact Mr. Johnson and see if he could obtain any fingerprints or other evidence left by the suspect. I doubted there would be any identifiable fingerprints because all surfaces appeared coated with dust, dirt, grease and oil…. but it was worth a try.

I watched how Craig handled himself and talked to Mr. Johnson as he collected the information for his report. Craig was polite and professional and called him "sir" or Mr. Johnson. In the days I spent with Craig, this was always his way with people and the other officers I encountered in the field were the same way.

This experience was something of an eye opener for me. Mr. Johnson was a black man and many, if not most, of the people we encountered as victims or suspects of crimes were black. Beat 29 was a minority neighborhood and a high crime area. I am embarrassed today to admit that I didn't expect my fellow police officers to treat black people the same way they treated white people. From newspapers and media reports through the years, I had been given the impression that police officers treated all black people poorly. I, the ignorant idealist fresh out of college, thought I would be a new breed of cop. I thought I would be making a difference and setting an example of racial impartiality, truth, justice and the American way. I had much to learn in my law enforcement career and learning about the fallible reliability and objectivity of the media was part of my education.

In 1966, black people were not called blacks, they were called negroes. In our training and police manuals, racism and racist terms were strictly prohibited. Among the terms, prohibited along with the "N word" was the term "black." We were prohibited from referring to negroes as blacks as it was considered racist. Times change and the term black evolved from a racist term to a term of racial pride. Ethnic terms for Italians and other people groups were also listed. Times and terms change.

I worked with Craig for a couple of weeks and eventually learned how to carry on a conversation with him while listening to the police radio in case we got a call. We always needed to keep an ear to the radio in order to know when we were being called, but also to have an idea of what was going on around us. When another officer made a car stop in our area, it was common to drive by and/or back up the officer in case there was trouble. If another officer on a car stop encounters a hostile subject or if the subject is determined to have warrants, it's common to call for a second officer to back him up. If an officer is sent to a potentially hazardous assignment, like a burglary alarm or a family fight, a second car is dispatched so at least two officers will be on the scene. The first car is the assigned officer, normally the beat officer, and the second car for backup, is called the "cover" car. It's common for officers to cover one another, even without being dispatched. Things can go wrong quickly, even on what appears to be a routine car stop, so we tended to look out for each other.

While working with Craig, we handled a wide variety of calls and incidents. We took many types of reports, handled family disturbances, responded to burglar alarms and all the typical things police officers do. While I remember the first call Craig and I responded to on my first night on the street, I don't remember everything else we did on that first night. However, I do remember I was wired at the end of the shift when we went off duty.

I ran into three other guys from the academy who were also getting off duty after their first night on the street. They were equally wired and invited me to join them for a beer as we recounted our first night as working police officers. It was around midnight and I was hyped and not sleepy, so I joined them for a beer while we recounted our experiences. I never did this again. I decided having a beer was not the best way to decompress after work and could develop into a bad habit. I felt I should have gone home to my wife rather than out with the guys. She would be asleep by the time I got home but that's where my life was. In years that followed, I found going home to decompress by reading a book in the quiet of the night worked best for me. By 1:30 or 2:00 a.m. I was usually decompressed enough to go to bed.

With the passage of time, memories fade and incidents blur but I still recall some memorable incidents while working with Craig. On one occasion we were dispatched to a family fight where the husband was threatening his wife. I was behind Craig when he knocked on the door. The door was opened quickly, and the angry husband stepped forward with a hammer raised above his head. Craig and I stepped back and drew our guns and the man quickly lowered the hammer and Craig took possession of it. He was drunk and we handled the matter without further incident. However, this incident reminded me to never approach a family fight in a routine way with my guard down.

We responded as a cover unit to a shooting one night and found a man down on the sidewalk in front of a store near 98th and Edes. He was angry and cursing at the police who were already on scene trying to find out who shot him and why. His shirt was up and there were two small holes in his fat stomach. There was little bleeding, but he had peed in his pants. He refused to cooperate and tell us who shot him and why. There were no witnesses willing or able to tell what happened. Craig and I weren't needed there and had a call elsewhere, so we left the scene after a short stay. The man died from his wounds and I don't know if the responsible party was ever identified.

On one occasion when responding to a burglary alarm, we chased down some subjects fleeing from the scene. I caught one, he was a teenager and to the amusement of some experienced fellow officers, I did my classic recruit school search before handcuffing him. It was the right thing to do but such procedures aren't always followed as rigorously by old salt officers – sometimes to their detriment.

Late one night Craig and I were on a meal break at a trucker cafe called the Double Clutch when we heard another unit being dispatched to a traffic accident not far from our location. As we concluded our meal break, we went to the nearby traffic accident to see if help was needed to direct traffic around the scene. A car with three or four people in it had stopped at a traffic light and a drunk driver rear ended their car. The collision caused the stopped car's gas tank to rupture, and the interior of the car was immediately engulfed in flame and everybody burned to death. Burned bodies are terrible to see and smell as they stretch out and extend their limbs in a macabre way as they burn. It was a horrible scene that I remember too well today. Fortunately, it was late at night and traffic wasn't a problem, we were not needed so we moved on.

After my couple weeks with Craig, I was assigned to work with Bill on beat 20. Bill was also a friendly and professional officer. However, the first thing he said to me when I got in the car with him on my first night was, "don't touch anything." He would drive the car and I would watch and learn. After about a week, Bill would allow me to do the talking and write the reports and this gave me more confidence.

Beat 20 was located toward mid-East Oakland and had a slightly different flavor than beat 29. It was a busy beat like 29 but it was mixed rather than predominantly minority in composition. In addition to all the usual stuff, I did have some memorable experiences when working with Bill.

One night, well after dark, we joined the pursuit of a stolen car that had just been involved in an armed robbery. The stolen car was well ahead of the pursuing car and blew through a red light on 35th avenue at MacArthur in front of us. Bill was driving and we took pursuit. The suspect car had a good lead and made a right turn off of 35th avenue and up a side street that was steeply uphill in a residential area. As we caught up and made a right turn to follow, the suspect car had been abandoned and was rolling backwards toward us. Bill turned into it and allowed the suspect's car to run into us to prevent it from rolling uncontrolled down the street. We jumped out quickly to inspect the suspect car to make sure nobody was in it. It was empty but further up the street we heard dogs barking as the suspects were fleeing through yards. We called in other units to block off adjacent streets to see if we could locate the suspects, but they had escaped.

On another evening, while it was still light, we were dispatched to a shooting. A caller had phoned the police and said he just shot his wife. The dispatcher told us that he was instructed to lay the gun down before the officers arrive. When we arrived at the address the husband was sitting on the front steps and the dead wife was laying on her back, partly out the front door. There was a significant wound and a lot of blood in her chest. We stepped over the body found a 3030-rifle leaning against a chair in the front room. It was a sad sight and I remember the look of grief on the husband's face. He admitted the shooting and we sent him off the jail.

I found that the greatest impact of dangerous, gruesome, and sad scenes and events is experienced after the fact. During these events, you have a job to do, and you are following protocols and procedures and focusing on what needs to be done. The greater impact comes when you try to process things hours, days, or weeks later. Often you find yourself processing things over and over and thinking, I should have done this or that or I could have done something better.

Toward the end of my ride-along training, it entered my mind that I might not survive my career all the way to retirement. My experiences on the street were unlike anything I had experienced before; this isn't what "normal" people do. There were real hazards almost every day and I wasn't used to this. I was chasing burglars in the night, rushing code 3 (red lights and siren) through the streets in pursuit of armed robbers, responding to family fights, burglaries, robberies and murders and encountering people who were hostile to me because I was a policeman. I had thought of myself as a "good guy" who wanted to remove "bad guys" from the community, so why did so many people hate me? I was hopelessly naïve. The job isn't just about good guys and bad guys, it's more complicated than that and I had to adjust my thinking. Over time I adjusted to the physical hazards of the job and came to realize the greater hazards were not to my physical being. More on this later.

After a few weeks working with Bill, I must have been deemed qualified to work alone. A Personnel Order came out and I found I was being transferred to first watch. First watch is the first shift of the day and we usually called it *dogwatch*. I don't know how it got that name but it sure fits. I always hated dogwatch; it was for the dogs as far as I was concerned.

In 1966, all Patrol watches rotated every three weeks. First watch rotated to third watch, third watch rotated to day watch and day watch rotated to first watch. With each rotation you had at least 8 hours after ending one shift and beginning another shift. The frequent rotation cycle took a toll on us so, after a few years the rotation cycles were changed to six-week intervals. This allowed more time for us to adjust to our sleep-wake cycles and stabilize our circadian rhythms. I dreaded the rotation from working days (second watch) to first watch (12:00 a.m. to 8:30 a.m.). Getting off at 4:30 p.m. and reporting back to work at 12:00 a.m. was difficult for everyone. I swore that sometimes when I was driving home at the end of day shift, I passed myself going the other way to work midnights.

Toward the end of my career the shift assignments no longer rotated and were determined by an annual draw based on seniority. In my opinion, this was not a good move. While having a steady shift was desirable in many respects, the downside was that people with low seniority usually ended up on the first or third watch while the senior officers ended up on day shift. There's an advantage to having senior (experienced) and new officers working the same shift together. On the other hand, it's nice for seniority to have some benefits so my opinion was a minority position. The seniority draw did work well for me when I returned to Patrol late in my career as a lieutenant. I had enough seniority to draw the day shift which was always my preference.

CHAPTER 5

WORKING SOLO

I had never worked a midnight shift in my life before reporting to lineup on my first shift on first watch which was also my first occasion to be working solo. I expected I might get tired, so I had tried to get some sleep in the evening before leaving the house to report to work at 12:00 midnight. Sleep was out of the question; I was excited to be on my own and apprehensive as well. I was awake and alert when I replied, "here sir" when my name was called at lineup and was told I was assigned to work beat 22. I would be 1L22 on my first night working solo.

After lineup, I walked the tunnel under 6th street to the Transportation Section where I located the car assigned to beat 22, loaded my gear and did my inspection. I hopped on the freeway heading toward beat 22 in East Oakland, picked up my radio microphone, pressed the *push to talk* button and advised dispatch "1L22 909D." This was the code we used to advise dispatch who we were and that we were on duty and available for assignment.

Oakland used the police 9 code system during my tenure. Most departments used the 10 code but somehow Oakland started and stuck with the 9 code. Every department tends to customize the codes they use but the 9 code and 10 code have commonalities. In the 9 code, as we used it, 909 meant you were done with the current assignment and available for the next. We used 909D to say we were coming on duty and available for assignment. At the end of the shift, we would advise that we were 908D; 908 told dispatch we were out of service and D meant going off duty.

In addition to memorizing all the various penal and vehicle codes and city ordinances we used, I had to learn how to use the police radio. While it's quite simple in practice, when everything is new you have to think before you act. When going on duty you had to select the proper radio channel to use based on which sector you would be working in the city. While most people today are used to push-to-talk buttons because of CB or toy walkie-talkies, I had never used a radio before and I had to remember to press the push-to-talk first, then talk, then immediately release the push-to-talk so you can hear dispatch respond to your call. It's all very simple but, if you've never done it before you have to force yourself to think: press push-to-talk, talk, release push-to-talk, listen for response. If you keep your push-to-talk button depressed, your radio will continue to transmit whether you are talking or not. As long as you are transmitting you cannot hear dispatch and other officers can't transmit because you are already using the channel. One of the common problems in police radio systems is what is called an *open mike*. This usually happens when an officer places his microphone on the seat rather than hanging it on the hook provided. The officer's gear on the seat can accidentally press the push-to-talk button and the radio channel is jammed until the problem is discovered. A mechanical malfunction can, in theory, jam a mike open but almost always the problem is organic (officer error) rather than electromechanical.

On my first solo shift I was assigned to a beat I had never worked before. When assigned to a new beat I would study the written description of beat boundaries and try to drive the boundaries and main streets in the beat to become familiar with them. Typically, I would be given an assignment before I could complete this and would often have to use a street guide (map) to find the location of my assignment. Over time as one becomes more familiar with Oakland's street geography you are able to respond without first referencing a street guide for every call. All patrol vehicles were equipped with spotlights and you quickly find it is very handy and sometimes necessary in order to locate street signs at night. As time went on, I found I frequently drove with my hand on the spotlight handle so I could inspect dark places and alleys as I drove about my beat in the dark of night. I'm probably not different from other officers but I found that when assigned to a beat I felt a certain responsibility to protect it, look for suspicious activity and to make my presence known to bad guys. The spotlight played a role in this.

I congratulated myself for finding my beat on that first night alone and began my patrol routine. I don't recall any particular calls for service I responded to that night but there would have been some for sure. The first few hours of dogwatch are typically busy but after 4:00 a.m. things typically, but not always, slowed down. When calls for service and radio traffic slowed down in the wee hours of the morning, for the first time in my life, I ran into the brick wall of fatigue. I had never been so sleepy without the possibility of sleep in all my life. I was driving down streets lined with dark houses and I could imagine people sleeping inside, all snug in their beds. I imagined how wonderful it would be to just put my head on a pillow and rest for five minutes. Of course, I didn't dare shut my eyes for even a minute as I would fall asleep and not wake up. I rolled my window down and took a deep breath of cool night air, but it didn't help. When I worked dogwatch, I would think of sleep in the way I imagined a starving person would think of food. It was a difficult struggle for me that first night and dogwatch continued to be difficult for me throughout my career.

As time went on, I found ways to cope with dogwatch, but I remember driving home after work with windows down in the winter and slapping my face to keep alert. During my shift I could always find an all-night café where I could get a cup of coffee but that didn't help for long and all-night cafes aren't known for good coffee. In those days, Oakland had a few 24-hour-a-day drive-ins called Doggie Diners. They were identified with a large plastic hound's head above the café. They always had coffee and it was always bad but, in desperate times, it was better than nothing. When I got my first cup of Doggie Diner coffee it entered my mind that I could charge them with assault with a caustic chemical for serving that stuff. Over time, however, a Doggie Diner at four in the morning looked like an oasis and I wondered if I might find a way to rig an IV drip using their coffee.

Sleeping at home during the day after working a dogwatch shift was difficult. My day was upside down. When everyone else is going to sleep, I'm going to work. When I'm trying to sleep, everyone else is out and about. While I'm struggling to find sleep, the neighbor kids are outside playing and making noise and neighbors are mowing their lawns. The noises of the neighborhood and light coming through the window tell you that you should be up, but your body is telling you, "no way."

While working dog watch, it seemed my life shrunk. There was a time to work and a time to try to sleep with very little life in between. The time between trying to sleep and going back to work was numb. On my days off I would try to live a normal life, being awake during the day and sleeping at night, but it interrupted my sleep cycle and there was a price to pay when I went back to work. Still, it was worth it to have a couple somewhat "normal" days during the week. I was fortunate to have a very accommodating wife who helped in every way for us to have as normal a life as possible. Later, when we had our daughter, she did an amazing job of keeping her quiet so I could sleep.

Eventually, I found some coping mechanisms that helped me survive dogwatch. Light blocking window shades helped some. I learned to eat a good breakfast when I got home and before going to bed. Even if not hungry I learned that I had to eat something before trying to sleep. If I didn't eat something I would wake up after a short while with my stomach growling. Val made some great homemade granola, and I found a good bowl of that worked well for me. It was sort of like a bear swallowing a pinecone before hibernating. It gave my stomach something to do while I slept. Even though I would get to bed around 9:30 or 10:00 a.m., I would often wake up around 1:00 to 3:00 p.m. I learned to not fight it. Rather than lying there fretting about being tired but unable to sleep, I got up... fumbled through the next few hours but went back to bed after dinner for an hour or two of sleep before going to work. I found that taking vitamin B12 helped me stay more alert during my shift. My wife, bless her heart, almost always made a sack lunch I could take to work. I would eat light to minimize the tiredness that follows a big meal.

It was always a little confusing to me. What do you eat at mid-shift around 4:00 a.m.? Normally mid-shift is lunch time but what meal do you eat at 4:00 a.m.? Is it lunch or breakfast? If I didn't have a sack lunch it was often difficult to decide what to eat at that hour. How about a Doggie Diner chili dog washed down with their caustic coffee? That was sure to be tasty and was equally sure to keep me awake for the rest of the shift.... and perhaps when I was trying to sleep when I got home.

For a number of weeks, I bounced around on the watch I was assigned to. Eventually we rotated to third watch and I continued with the same crew. I was used to plug holes to fill a beat where an officer was off for a day or sick. I worked a number of different beats at different locations around the city. I was also assigned to be the second officer on the paddy wagon a few times. On this assignment we drove around the city picking up prisoners from officers and transporting them to jail.

I was amazed to find the diversity in the types of calls I was dispatched to handle. Every day was different, and I never know what would be in front of me when I start my shift. Most assignments dealt with common crimes like assault, burglary, robbery or theft but some were out of the ordinary. I particularly disliked handling suicides. They had a sadness that exceeded a homicide in my mind. I remember one suicide where a young man about my age shot himself in the head. I wondered why did he do this, what drove him to this? If I had been there, could I have said something to him that would have made a difference? Many assignments left me with unanswered questions.

One day watch I was sent to investigate a lady sitting in a parked car in a commercial area for a long time. Someone had noticed this and called the police. On arrival, I saw a young lady about my age sitting behind the steering wheel with a small bloody wound on her chest. She was wearing a thick raincoat and was obviously dead. I didn't see a suicide note or a weapon, so I began to handle the call as a homicide. When the coroner removed the body from the car, they found the gun she had used in the large inside pocket of her raincoat. Upon shooting herself, the gun she used had dropped into the pocket. A suicide note was found later. It was always sad to see a relatively young person take their life.

Responding to family disturbances was a common assignment. You have to remind yourself that they are never routine. Many officers were injured when responding to family disturbances. I was surprised to find how often a woman will stay living with a man who is abusive to her. Even when the man is arrested for assault it seems so often they get back together. Occasionally a family fight that starts as an argument ends in a homicide. I responded to one family disturbance where on arrival I found the female had shot the male in the head. It's difficult to refer to so many couples as husband and wife because the formality of marriage is often neglected in dysfunctional relationships. It was evident that the "wife" had shot the "husband" in the head because he said so. He had possession of the gun and pointed to an entrance wound on the left side of his head. I also noticed an exit wound on the upper right side of his head. I wasn't used to carrying on a coherent conversation with someone shot in the head, so it took us some time to figure out what happened. The bullet had entered at an upward angle on the left side of the head and traveled under the skin over the top of the head and exited on the upper right side of the head. So ended another "routine" family disturbance. The wife goes to jail, the husband goes to the hospital and the gun goes into evidence. Usually, it's the husband that goes to jail but not this time.

I was dispatched to investigate a reported vandalism one day shift. On arrival, an elderly lady took me outside and showed me the vandalism to her house. It consisted of some dry rot and aged peeling paint. She said it was new last week and was convinced someone had vandalized her house. I assured her I would make a report and took her back inside her house and talked to her about her next of kin and managed to call her son and explain the situation to him. I wasn't familiar with Alzheimer's at the time but attributed it to age related mental deterioration.

A fellow officer told me how he was dispatched to a call when an elderly lady called to report that her husband might be sick and need an ambulance. It turned out that her husband was in bed, but he wasn't sick. He had been dead for weeks and was somewhat mummified. She had been sleeping with him and even put some food in his mouth. The job can be incredibly sad sometimes.

I was sent to a location to meet a lady who was having an undetermined problem with her husband. On arrival at the location an older lady came up to me and pointed to a car and house telling me that the car was her husband's, and the house was his girlfriend's house. She was in tears and clung to me as I awkwardly explained that there was nothing I could do in this situation – it wasn't a police matter. I told her to seek the counsel of her pastor. Some calls leave you feeling worthless.

Eventually I was assigned to a relief squad. A relief squad is a group of officers and a sergeant who work a district when the regular personnel assigned to that district are on their days off. Every district was staffed by a group of officers and a sergeant who all had the same days off together.

Filling in in this way was fine with me as I liked working in different locations around the city rather than being assigned to the same beat every day.

During this early period on the Oakland Police Department Val and I moved around Oakland a few times. We initially had a furnished apartment on McClure street but we found a better priced small unfurnished place on Mandana Blvd. We bought a cheap refrigerator, a bed, a dining table with chairs and a few items of furniture at a used furniture store. We carried our chairs from the dining table in the kitchen to the living room in order to sit and watch our used black and white television set. We lived frugally but we were saving money in order to one day own a house. After a few months, the owner-manager of the apartment told us we had to leave when he noticed that Val was pregnant. He said he didn't want the noise associated with a child in the house. He lived downstairs and we lived upstairs. We moved to a duplex on 34th avenue where another officer, a friend from recruit school and his family lived below, and we lived above. We were living there when our daughter was born.

These were eventful times. A new job with varying hours with physical and psychological adjustments, multiple moves, a new daughter and all the adjustments newly married couples go through. Nevertheless, I wasn't different from the other young officers I attended the academy with. Police officers have lives apart from the job with families and the typical duties, cares and problems of life.

CHAPTER 6

A REGULAR ASSIGNMENT

It felt good to be given a regular assignment. I was assigned to what we called a relief crew and would be working with a sergeant supervisor and a group of officers in districts where the regular assigned personnel were on their days off. This also gave me regular days off, another advantage to plan my life around.

My work week started on Friday when I was assigned to beat 22 in mid-East Oakland. On Saturday and Sunday, I was assigned to beat 8 which was in north-Oakland bordering Berkeley and Emeryville. On Monday and Tuesday, I worked beat 2 which was in downtown commercial Oakland. Beat 2 usually had two officers assigned to it, a 2A and a 2B. I was assigned to be 2B if you pardon the pun. This made Wednesday and Thursday my regular days off. Having days off mid-week has advantages and disadvantages but having regular days off for an extended period of time made it easier to make life plans.

Rotating shifts with mid-week days off made it difficult to coordinate social events with others but you learn to adjust and manage. Going to church was a priority for us and we managed that. In those days, churches usually had a morning and an evening service so I could almost always manage to attend one or the other.

Vacations were allocated by seniority draw. The senior officers snatched up the good summer and holiday vacations, so for many years I ended up with winter vacations. January, February and March were typically available for someone with my seniority. With my seniority, if a holiday like Christmas fell on my normal day off I was lucky but more often than not, I worked most holidays. I was hard pressed to complain as we had three weeks of vacation every year and I felt fortunate for that. Rotating shifts, mid-week days off and winter vacations were not optimum but I was happy to have a job with good pay. I started at $663 a month, and while that looks pathetic today, it was a good salary in 1966.

People would often ask my wife, Valerie, how she coped with me working as a police officer in Oakland. Oakland was not known for a lack of crime. We were Christians and Val always told others that she had confidence in the Lord and trusted Him for my safety. She was confident she could handle whatever might happen through her faith in the Lord. Even so, I decided early on not to tell Val everything that happened or that I did during a tour of duty. She might ask, "How did it go today?" I would usually answer with, "Not much," or "Just the usual." The exciting or hazardous events in the line of duty became what we called "sea stories." Sea stories were mostly reserved to be shared with other officers. Sea stories were not for wives.

Early on in my career I would think, "Someday I should write a book about this." I found some other new officers were thinking the same way. The things we experienced on a regular basis were amazing, exciting and new and sometimes sad or funny. These aren't things most people experience so writing about them when they were new to us seemed like a good idea. However, over time, what was exciting, new, sad or funny became part of a regular day's work. It was no longer new or unusual, it was routine, and nobody is inclined to write about what is routine. I did keep a scrap book for a while but most of us grew out of the idea that we should write a book about our experiences on the streets of Oakland.

I am writing today about my experience in law enforcement after many years of retirement. With this distance I feel I can write with greater insight and objectivity after I have had sufficient time to decompress. If I had written a book in the early stages of my career, it would have been front-loaded with the drama of the job but without the perspective that comes with a full career. Now that I have stepped back from the job, I feel I have something to share with people who have only looked at police work and police officers from the outside. Today, I can share the inside from the outside.

Over time in my relief crew assignment working beats 22, 8 and 2, I became more familiar with the people and geography of each beat. Each beat had a slightly different flavor. Beat 22 was mostly residential and 8 was also mostly residential but with a good mix of commercial and industrial. Beat 2 was in the downtown commercial area. The typical calls for service differed from beat to beat and the types of criminal activity we were hoping to prevent differed also. The flavor of each beat also differed by hour of day (shift) so I appreciated the physical and social differences of each beat.

I continued to feel a sort of Boy Scout responsibility to prevent crime and catch bad guys on any beat to which I was assigned. When not responding to a family fight, taking a burglary report or investigating a traffic accident, I attempted to present a police omnipresence effect by actively patrolling the streets on my beat. I made a point to not patrol in a predictable pattern and would try to be random in my patrols while frequenting known trouble spots.

Oakland is a high crime city, so I took lots of reports of burglaries, robberies, assaults, thefts, etc. I found it frustrating as a police officer to take reports after the fact and not being there at the time to catch the perpetrator. I don't think I'm different from any other officer in that my goal was to prevent crime and catch the bad guy in the act. I was much happier to respond to a report of a burglary or robbery in progress than to take what we called a cold report after-the-fact. With a crime in progress, I had an opportunity to catch the bad guy or at least find a witness who could give me a description. In most after-the-fact burglary and theft reports there is no witness or suspect description. With a suspect description we at least knew who we were looking for. Taking report after report with no known suspect is powerful incentive to catch the bad guy and bring him to justice; even knowing that justice can be as elusive as the suspect.

When responding to a just-occurred crime with a witness, the first priority was to get the best possible description of the suspect so you could broadcast it to other officers in the area. When a crime in progress is reported, more than one officer is dispatched to the scene. The primary officer, usually the beat officer, will go to the scene, take the report and broadcast the suspect description but other available officers will patrol surrounding streets searching for the fleeing suspect. I loved responding to a just-occurred crime with a suspect description. Here was a chance to catch the criminal rather than just take a report. Catching a perpetrator rather than just taking a report provided a sense of satisfaction and was an opportunity to prevent further crime. Taking after-the-fact reports, day after day you meet and deal with many victims of crime. Catching a perpetrator makes you feel good about your job. You felt you did something worthwhile for the victims and it gave you bragging rights in the locker room at the end of the shift.

I will take this opportunity to explain one of the inherent difficulties and frustrations that comes with the job. When responding to a just occurred crime with a suspect description you are looking at cars and people that might match the broadcast description of the perpetrator. Every officer, at one time or another has captured a fleeing suspect in this process. The problem is, the officer might be looking for a fleeing armed robber and the person matching the description might be an innocent citizen in the area that just happens to look like the described perpetrator. The officer is within his or her legal rights to stop and detain such a person until it can be determined if he is actually the suspect. This determination will be made by questioning, clarifying the suspect description or bringing a witness by the location where the party is detained to determine if he is the actual suspect. If the person being detained is an innocent person who happened to be in the neighborhood you can understand their lack of appreciation for the police "service" they are receiving. If the person detained turns out to be the actual perpetrator, he's not happy with the police either but who cares, the victim is happy the police captured the perpetrator.

Now, let's look at this situation in the context of real-life Oakland and let's add the dynamic of race to the equation. Many areas of Oakland are populated by low-income blacks and are high crime areas. This means there are many black victims of crime and many black suspects of crime. Accordingly, police in these areas respond to many reports of crime in progress or just-occurred with a black suspect described. It follows that often the suspects that police encounter and detain as they respond to these crimes are innocent black citizens. From these encounters, many people claim that the police are "always" harassing blacks in their own neighborhoods. Some will say, "You just stopped me because I'm black." The truth is they were stopped because they were black and matched the description of a suspect in a just-occurred crime.

These are very dangerous situations because the officer may believe they are encountering an armed individual who just committed a violent crime, and they will have their weapon out when they make the detention. If the person detained is not the person who committed the crime and feels the police are just harassing him may be uncooperative. The officer with the right to detain a potentially dangerous uncooperative suspect is in a tough situation. Is the person uncooperative because he is the suspect or uncooperative because he thinks he is being unjustly harassed by the police?

This situation can arise with a black, white or an officer of any ethnicity, but it seems to be that people often look beyond the blue uniform to blame the color of the officer's skin. With an armed police officer and potentially armed uncooperative suspect, much can go wrong. In my experience, explaining the reason for the detention of an uncooperative suspect does little to defuse the situation. Sometimes the uncooperative detained suspect is the actual perpetrator and sometimes it's an innocent passerby.

If police were to make no effort to capture fleeing suspects in predominantly black neighborhoods, they would avoid these situations, but they would do the victims of crime no justice. Blacks have a right to live in safe communities, but the police are seen by some to be the enemy. Still, the majority of the people in black community want the police there for their protection.

One of my favorite crime-in-progress calls was early in my career when I was working beat 2, the downtown beat during day watch. The call went out for a bank robbery alarm at 715 Broadway. This was within a block of the police department, so the robber didn't research the job well. A paddy wagon was close to the scene and was able to quickly broadcast a description and direction of flight of the suspect. I was familiar enough with the beat to anticipate where the suspect might be going and turned the wrong way down a one-way street and soon saw the suspect running toward me. He apparently didn't expect me to be going the wrong way toward him on the street in spite of the fact that someone blew their horn at me. He didn't notice me until I jumped out of the car with my gun drawn and told him to freeze and put his hands in the air. He was startled and put his hand in his right coat pocket. He was wearing a navy P coat which matched the description broadcast by the paddy wagon. Realizing he had put his hand in his pocket, while pointing my gun at him from about 8 feet I ordered him to take his hand out of his pocket and put his hands in the air. (I think I may have cussed for emphasis.) He removed his hand from his pocket, and I watched closely to see that it was empty. It was empty so I placed him against the wall to his right and searched him finding his loaded gun in the pocket where he had put his hand. This is why it's important to watch the hands when arresting or confronting a subject on the street. In his left coat pocket was a cloth bag with money from the bank in it and a note saying, "this is a holdup." I had not received FBI training at this point, but I took this to be a clue that I had arrested the right guy.

I arrested the 18-year-old subject for bank robbery, and he was sent to the gray-bar hotel. Apparently, his time in prison did not fully rehabilitate him as some 12 years later he was charged with robbery and murder in connection with a body found in the trunk of a car at the Oakland Airport.

Not long after going to the street, I realized that I needed glasses. This was particularly apparent when working nights. Even with my spotlight I found it difficult to read street signs. Reading street signs and addresses on the fly is extremely important because a police officer must not only know where he is going but where he is at every moment while on patrol. If you are not paying attention to where you are, you will be in trouble in the event you encounter a crime in progress or need help for whatever reason. To get the help or backup you need, you will have to be able to tell dispatch where you are so help can be sent. It does little good to call for help if you can't tell anybody where you are. When on patrol you always make note of the street you are on, so it was soon evident that I needed glasses to help me read street signs and addresses.

Going into college I had 20-20 vision but the heavy reading requirements in college caused my eyesight to deteriorate. When I obtained glasses, they made a big difference, especially at night. Even after I got glasses, I remember turning onto a street named "Ygnatio" and hoping I didn't need help while on this street as I wasn't familiar with Spanish pronunciations at the time and had no idea how to pronounce the street if I had to call for assistance.

For the first few years on the department, we didn't have portable radios. If we needed to call for help, we had to use the car radio. Unfortunately, much of the time we were out of the car and in a residence or pursuing a suspect through back yards and if you needed to call for help you were out of luck. To get help you would have to go back to your car and turn the engine on before the radio would work. This was not a good situation given the nature of police work. It was a great relief when we all got portable radios that we could use wherever we were. Not only was it helpful for officer safety but it enabled us to broadcast suspect descriptions in real time rather than obtaining a description then going back to your car to broadcast it. Soon after we obtained portable radios, we couldn't imagine working without them.

My wife and I had started saving money as soon as I came on the police department. Our goal was to buy a house of our own. After a couple years we had saved enough for a down payment and we decided to buy a new house in Livermore, CA. It meant a long commute for me, but Livermore had a small town feel and was an easy drive to the country. We both had our roots in the country or small towns, so it fit us well. New houses in safe neighborhoods were more affordable in Livermore and it did not have a high crime reputation. I took crime reports all day long in Oakland and had parts stolen off my personal car at our place on 34th Avenue so buying a house in Livermore appealed to us in many ways.

Working my three beats on the relief squad was a good fit for me. Day shifts usually started slow but got busy by mid-morning. Third watch, the evening shift, tended to be busy much of the time. First watch (dogwatch) was busy till after the bars closed at 2:00 a.m., but usually slowed down after 4:00 a.m. The slow time after 4:00 a.m. was often quite difficult because your lack of sleep caught up with you during those hours. By the time the sun came up and people started commuting to work I was dreaming about a pillow and trying to stay out of everyone's way while trying to keep my eyes open. I was always happy to see the end of a long dogwatch shift.

During these rookie years I recall handling my first fatal vehicle accident. It was dispatched as a possible 901A (vehicle accident with injuries). On arrival, I found a VW bug was the only vehicle involved and it had run into a construction abutment. There wasn't a terrible amount of damage so as I approached the vehicle, I looked among the people standing around to see anyone would step forward as the driver. When I looked inside the vehicle there were two dead people. The driver had crushed his chest on the steering wheel which was bent, and the passenger had gone face first through the windshield which cut her throat. She was crumpled on the floor on the passenger side with her head back on the seat where she had been sitting. Blood flowed from her front seat to pool on the floor in the back seat. I called for an ambulance and checked for vital signs but found none. The car hadn't been going very fast, but it hit an absolutely immovable abutment and that's all it took. It was traumatic and stuck with me for years. I handled a few murders and shooting working those beats, but most were not as memorable as the first fatal accident. It taught me something about driver safety and using seatbelts.

Some other calls were unique for one reason or another. One swing shift I was dispatched to a location where someone had called the police reporting that someone was yelling for help in a smaller residence in the rear of a larger house. On arrival, the people in the house at the front directed me to the house at the rear. When I went inside, I found a man lying on the floor yelling in pain. He had a huge bloody hole in his hip and there was blood and tissue dripping down the wall next to him. I asked him what happened, and he angrily said he didn't know. He said he heard a loud bang and the next thing he knew he was on the floor. I called for an ambulance and looked around and didn't see a weapon or anything he or anyone could use to cause this injury. I had no idea what had happened and neither did the poor guy with the wound. A sergeant arrived at about the time an ambulance hauled the injured party away. We looked around and noticed an open window and a very small hole in the window screen which was on the side of the house facing the house in front. We guessed that a bullet had come through that screen and hit the man. Some detectives arrived at this time and the sergeant sent me to follow up with the victim at the hospital. I learned later that someone in the house in front was playing with a rifle and claimed he accidentally shot through the window of the house in back. I never learned what happened in court.

I was dispatched to a 415F (code for family disturbance) late one night and found a lady lying on her back at the bottom of the front steps of her house with both forearms broken and bent at an angle. A man standing nearby was bleeding from deep slashes in both arms and hands. The story we got was this. They had both gone to bed when the lady told the man to get up and turn out the hall light. The man refused to do it and an argument ensued. The argument escalated to the point where she obtained a butcher knife (which I found lying on the ground near her) and started attacking the man who picked up a 2x4 board and started swinging it at her. She cut him up badly and he broke both her arms. With the heat of the battle over by the time I arrived, they were both saying, "I'm sorry baby…I love you." I called for an ambulance and sent them both off to the hospital swearing their love for each other. Family fights are unpredictable and can escalate from a small thing to a homicide. Alcohol is often a factor and they can be dangerous to the officer who responds.

It was common for the police to be dispatched to investigate when people call for an ambulance. Often the call for an ambulance is the result of a crime or some sort of violence. When working dogwatch, I hated to get the ambulance requested call at 5:00 or 6:00 a.m. It was often when one spouse wakes up in the morning to find the other spouse has passed away in the night. These were sad situations, but we were required to make a preliminary investigation and complete an "unexplained death" report.

I received an assignment to check to see if an ambulance was required at a location on San Pablo Avenue one day shift. Someone had called dispatch and said there was a man there that may need an ambulance. On arrival there was an older man sitting in a chair in a vacant lot near a sign that said, "Bad Dog." I had seen the sign and the man in the chair there on many occasions, he was something like a permanent fixture in the lot. My information was that the man in the chair may need an ambulance, so I approached him and asked him how he was doing. He was heavily intoxicated and hard to understand so I asked him if he was in need of an ambulance. He reached down and started to pull up his pants leg at which time I saw maggots dripping down his leg and over his foot. He had a large maggot-infested injury on his leg, so he got his ambulance.

One of the assignments I dreaded was "hospital guard." When a prisoner charged with a serious crime was sent to the hospital but still physically capable of escape, an officer was assigned to guard the prisoner to prevent escape during hospital treatment. This is a miserable assignment at any time but particularly miserable during dogwatch. This assignment usually involved an early and a late assigned officer, each officer was required to stand guard for four hours. My greatest dread was to get the late hospital guard assignment on dogwatch. This meant that from 4:00 a.m. to 8:00 a.m., I would have to sit in a chair in the dark or dimly lit doorway of a hospital room where the prisoner was sleeping. While sitting in the dark with everybody around me sleeping I had to fight off sleep myself while guarding a prisoner who was sleeping comfortably in a bed. This was agony.

One eventful night, in the wee hours of the morning, I was working beat 8, when I got a call off my beat to meet my sergeant at a location on 61st Street. The sergeant took me inside a house and opened the refrigerator in the kitchen and pointed to a tumbler filled with a yellowish liquid. The sergeant said it was nitroglycerine and enough to blow up the house and possibly the neighbor houses which had been evacuated.

Apparently, the father in the house discovered his 18-year-old son up and working in the kitchen at 3:00 a.m. The son gently carried some liquid in a container and put it in the refrigerator telling his father it was nitroglycerine. The son was a straight A student in chemistry and the father saw a chemistry book on the kitchen table opened to the page dealing with nitroglycerine. No small argument ensued followed by a fight which the father won, after which he had called the police. The son went to jail for possession of explosives and the house and neighboring houses had been evacuated. A military bomb squad had been called to dispose of the nitroglycerine which was very unstable in that condition. The sergeant told me to sit in the car in front of the house and not let anybody into the house until the military bomb disposal people arrived. The sergeant said I would be relieved when the day shift came on duty and he left the scene.

About an hour later, as I sat in the dark in my car in front of the house with the nitroglycerine, I heard the police radio traffic of a gun battle between the sergeant and a couple of suspects who had been under surveillance for various crimes including kidnapping. In the shootout the sergeant was shot three times and a second officer was also hit. A third officer charged the scene firing his weapon and the suspects were wounded and taken into custody. Nobody died in the shootout, but the sergeant carried a bullet in his hip for the rest of his career.

About a year later, the young man who concocted the nitroglycerin ran a stop sign late one night while driving at high speed and was pursued by an Oakland police officer. The pursuit took the officer out of radio contact beyond the city limits behind hills on Redwood Road and ended when the young man lost control of his car on a curve and ended up on a dirt embankment. As the officer approached, the young man opened fire on the officer with a .45 pistol, hitting the officer twice. Fortunately, none of the rounds hit a bone and the officer returned fire. The officer's rounds missed the subject who had emptied his gun and dropped it to surrender. The officer, with an empty gun and two bullet wounds, handcuffed the subject and placed him in the back of his police car. The officer drove his prisoner back to the City of Oakland where he was back in radio contact and able to call for assistance. The officer was seriously wounded but recovered and eventually returned to duty.

A majority of individuals I arrested for serious crimes had previous arrests. This was common. I noticed that many times while I was sitting the front seat of my patrol car writing a report connected with an arrestee in the back seat, the arrestee would just go to sleep. This is how traumatic it was for some when arrested for a serious crime. A very few shed tears when arrested but I can only recall one occasion when the tears appeared to be tears of remorse.

It does some damage to one's idealistic sense of justice to realize that we are often arresting perpetrators committing crimes for which they have been previously arrested and perhaps were already on probation or parole for. I never did the math on it, but it seemed that if certain repeat offenders were kept in prison and off the street, the crime rate would be significantly diminished. The frustration was increased when a case went to trial and the individual you knew was guilty was let off on a technicality. It sometimes seemed that I, the arresting officer, was on trial rather than the perp. Did I do everything right? Did I "dot" every "i" and cross every "T?" The fact at issue in court seemed to be anything but guilt or innocence. I realized that our system of justice rightly requires police officers to comply with laws relating to arrest, search and seizure but these laws seemed to be ever changing and interpreted in favor of the arrestee. After working all night and then going to court all day to see a person you know is guilty get off on a technicality or through what you feel is unjustified leniency takes a toll on one's enthusiasm. The perpetrator gets the benefit of the doubt, but what about all the victims? I had heard the expression that says, "The wheels of justice turn slowly but they grind fine." I learned a cynical variation of this saying that went like this, "The wheels of justice turn slowly but they are sure fouled up."

While the realities of the street and criminal justice system were at odds with my idealistic thinking, I realized at another level that, even with its inefficiencies, the American justice system was one of the best in the world. I would certainly prefer the inefficiencies of the American justice system to the efficiencies of a totalitarian state. The idealistic concepts of justice and rehabilitation get a bit fuzzy in the workings of our justice system so one learns to temper idealism with reality. I tended to think of myself as part of the solution to crime and criminality in society, but it often seemed that I was considered part of the problem.

Perhaps one example might help explain my frustration. In the wee hours of dogwatch one day, another officer and I were dispatched to check out a situation where a citizen had called in to report that two guys in a particular car were acting suspiciously. The area could be described as high crime where narcotic activity was common. When we arrived, we found two guys sitting in the dark in the described car. We asked them to step out and proceeded to pat them down for weapons to ensure our safety.

On a similar previous occasion when I was dispatched to check out suspicious individuals in a car, I asked one of the occupants to step out of the car while we determined who they were and why they were in the area. Someone had thought them suspicious enough to call the police, so we were checking them out. I asked the individual for identification and as he was going to hand it to me it fell out of his hand to the sidewalk. I wasn't about to bend down in front of him so I stepped back so he could pick up his driver's license. When he bent down to pick up his license, his concealed pistol fell out of his pocket onto the sidewalk. There was a second gun in the car. You don't know who you are dealing with in these situations.

My point is that we were legally justified under the circumstances to pat the "suspicious" individuals down for weapons. When I ran my hand down the outside of my subject's leg I felt a loose lump in his sock. When I felt it, I "knew" from experience that it was a balloon of heroin. Heroin is commonly wrapped for sale in a balloon forming a small ball. I asked the subject, "What's this?" He said, "Nothing," so I removed it and placed him under arrest for possession of narcotics. When the case went to court, I was questioned extensively on how many arrests I had made for heroin, why I thought it was a balloon of heroin, had I told the individual he was under arrest before removing the heroin, and so on. In the end, they threw the case out as an illegal search. The right to pat the individual down for weapons under the circumstances was not challenged but removing what turned out to be a balloon of heroin was successfully challenged on technical grounds. To this day I am confident it was a legal seizure and arrest. I had not told the subject he was under arrest before removing the heroin, but he was technically under arrest as I testified that he was not free to go at that point. The seizure from the sock was based on a *probable cause* technical arrest but that's how it goes in court sometimes. Spending my day off in court to watch an individual I know is guilty get off on a technicality made my sense of justice fuzzy.

For the reader not familiar with the term *probable cause* I will explain that a peace officer under California law can make an arrest for a crime in his presence or upon probable cause for certain serious crimes not in his presence. The officer doesn't need proof of guilt, that's determined in court, but probable cause essentially means is there a good reason to make the arrest. There was a court case around that time that defined probable cause as: "Such a state of facts that would lead a person of ordinary care and prudence to believe and conscientiously entertain an honest and strong suspicion that a crime has been committed." I memorized that definition to be able to roll it off my tongue in the event a defense attorney in court should ask me what I meant by probable cause. Much to my chagrin, I never got that opportunity.

I was in and out of a wide variety of homes during my time working the street. On a typical day I would visit more than one home to take some kind of police report. It could involve a burglary, theft, runaway juvenile, assault or any of a variety of matters. Most homes were neat and tidy as one would expect. However, I visited some homes that are memorable to this day because of their unbelievable filth. I have seen stovetops black with uncleaned spills and with spill streaks down the side of the stove and on counter tops refrigerators and, of course the floor. Sometimes there were stacks of unwashed dishes in the kitchen and various rooms along with piles of unwashed clothes on the floor in various rooms. I've seen dirty carpets with trails where people walked and clutter beyond imagination. Such homes are usually the habitat of a thriving cockroach population which the residents don't seem to notice. I've taken reports from people sitting in a chair or couch with cockroaches running around them on the furniture and across their bodies unnoticed. If one runs across their face, they brush it away like one would dispatch a mosquito. In such a home, I never sat down and would stand in the middle of a room while collecting the information I needed for my report. I would be sure to keep my feet moving to make myself a hard target for the cockroaches. Of course, there would be a noticeable stench in such homes. In winter months the stench would be magnified in some homes by the fact that the heat was on its highest setting and all the gas burners on the stove would be aflame at the highest setting. The residents would be wearing shorts and T-shirts in this tropical setting and I would be toasting inside my blue wool uniform. If I entered the house wearing a coat, I wouldn't dare take it off as I couldn't set it down lest it collect cockroach passengers.

In some homes where I would be taking a report there would be a young child, typically a boy, who would be fascinated with my uniform equipment. Often, they had difficulty keeping their hands off my gun belt that was loaded with many things of interest to a child. Initially I tried to ignore them as long as they kept their hands away from my gun but one day a child found the whistle hanging from my keyring and started blowing it. I really didn't need that, so I guarded the gun and my whistle after that.

The whistle on the belt was normally used for traffic control. However, one officer pursued a suspect into a dark location one night and was shot. He had given his general location but in the course of the pursuit had moved and officers responding to his location had difficulty locating him. He was down and able to talk on his radio but couldn't give his exact location, so he blew on his whistle which enabled officers to find him.

I was a slow learner when it came to kids and my equipment belt. One day, as I was interviewing his mother for a report of some sort, a child was fiddling with my belt away from the gun and whistle when he started to cry. At that same time, I smelled the unmistakable smell of my chemical mace. Chemical mace was essentially a liquid form of teargas in a canister carried in a leather case on my belt. As long as a child didn't unsnap the cover to the leather case that contained the mace, I didn't worry about it. However, this kid managed to slip a finger inside the leather case and press the button that released the chemical spray. He didn't get a direct hit but the mist that was released burned his eyes. I had his mother wash his face and eyes with cold water and the matter was adjusted but I had learned my lesson. No more mister nice guy. Keep your hands off my belt, kid.

Chemical mace was a useful tool in cases where deadly force was not justified. Almost every officer is sprayed by mace at some time. It typically happens when officers are struggling with a recalcitrant suspect and one of the officers will use mace on the subject to try to get him to stop struggling. However, in the process, any other engaged officers will get a splash-back dose or at least encounter some mist in the process.

I only used mace on someone once and it proved effective. I was working day watch on beat 8 and driving through a commercial area. It was a Sunday, so most businesses were closed but I heard glass breaking and a ringing burglar alarm activate. Being highly trained in such things, I deducted that a crime might be in progress. I advised radio of the situation and my location and exited the car to go around the back side of an office building where the sound was coming from. There I found a smashed window and a man standing next to it. I held him at gunpoint and ordered him to turn around. He refused to cooperate, and it was apparent that he had been drinking. He continued to refuse to cooperate, so I used my left hand (non-gun hand) to mace him in the face. He put his hands to his face and dropped to his knees. I was able to handcuff him at this point. Officers found that mace was not effective on all people in all circumstances. It seemed to have little effect on some people, especially when high on certain drugs.

While I only maced someone else once, I used it on myself on more than one occasion. I found that if I had a cold and my nasal passages were totally blocked, I could squirt a little mace on a finger and touch it between my eyes on my forehead and clear my sinuses quite well. A temporary burning sting and watering eyes was preferrable to blocked nasal passages. Needless to say, I didn't find this procedure in a training manual and I didn't do this at high noon at 12th and Broadway. I didn't have the good sense to stay home with a miserable cold, so I had to improvise.

CHAPTER 7

THE LIFE OF A BEAT COP

I don't want to just tell the reader sea stories about my experiences as a beat cop. I will tell some stories, but I want the reader to appreciate the stories in the demographic, social, and political context of the city, state, and nation at the time. The experiences officers have in the line of duty occur in a certain set of circumstances at a point in time, but they are not isolated from the greater cultural context. Law enforcement officers and the culture are both influenced, impacted, challenged, and changed by evolving social and political events and perspectives. Police officers often make decisions in a split second that will take a six-month trial to sort out in a political, social, and legal context.

Everybody is changed by their life experiences. The life experiences law enforcement officers encounter can be frustrating, intense, and traumatic on a scale above what the average person experiences in their work. These experiences will have an impact on individual officers and each officer must learn to deal with them in a healthy way. Most do, some don't. I can only describe what I experienced, how it impacted me and how I dealt with it.

The American justice system is built around the idea that it is better for a guilty person to go free than for an innocent person to be imprisoned. Who can argue with that concept? As in any imperfect manmade system, it gets complicated and even messy in the application of that concept in real life circumstances. Nevertheless, as a Christian, I came to grips with what

I saw as the injustices and inefficiencies of the justice system by reminding myself that man's justice is and always will be imperfect. God's justice, on the other hand is absolute. I reminded myself that Scripture tells us that "It is appointed unto men once to die, after this the judgement." (Hebrews 9:27) I told myself that I didn't need to obsess on the shortcomings of our justice system because, in the long run, we all must stand before God where justice is served. If I were to lie in court or produce false evidence to force what I thought was justice, I would be no better than the other criminals. So, I did my best to play the game by the rules and let the chips fall where they will.

We have one of the best justice systems in the world, but it is imperfect and run by fallible men and women. Accordingly, my confidence was in the fact that while there is often injustice in the short run, over a period of 100 years justice is absolute. I also reminded myself that even the vilest criminal can escape eternal punishment by accepting God's salvation by faith in Christ Jesus.... just as I did. It was and continues to be necessary to frequently remind myself of this perspective.

At the time I went on the streets as a rookie cop in the City of Oakland, California, there was a lot of turmoil in the country. There had been race riots in a number of large cities across the nation and the nation was engaged in an unpopular war in Viet Nam. The Black Muslim religion was often in the headlines nationally and was active in the Bay Area. On top of this, the Black Panther Party had been established in Oakland and would soon have a national reach. The Black Panther Party headquarters was on beat 8, one of my regular beats. In addition to this, there were various leftist terrorist groups in operation around the country and locally. Most of these groups were anti-police and even targeted police on occasion. This would become very clear to me over time.

I found policework to be a combination of interesting, exciting, terrifying, challenging, sickening, sad, frustrating, and boring. Every job produces a variety of experiences but in police work the experiences are intense and can come on rapidly. You could experience all of the emotions in my list on a single 8-and-a-half-hour shift but almost certainly you would experience them in any given work week.

Not long after I started working solo, the City of Oakland experienced some sporadic but widespread racial violence and vandalism. The exact cause of the violence was unclear but appeared to be related to an ad hock organization in support of "quality education" calling for a boycott of schools. The violence began with vandalism and teachers being assaulted in an East Oakland high school. Classes were suspended as a result of the violence and it spread beyond the school where it started. Hundreds of youngsters from various schools cut classes and violence occurred with black youths roaming the streets in small groups. Some violence continued into the night and there were many arrests of juveniles and adults. Days off were canceled at the police department and I was called to work.

I was paired with another officer and sent to patrol the streets of East Oakland to prevent vandalism from roving groups of juveniles. The streets were pretty quiet by that time, but we came upon a group of juveniles spraying something on a wall outside of Oakland High School. We caught them with spray paint in hand and saw that they had sprayed the worlds, "F(word) N(word)" and "White Power" on the wall. They admitted what they had done, and we arrested three youths involved in the vandalism. All were black and obviously attempting to fan the flames of racial dissent.

As I describe incidents I was involved in, I won't normally describe the race of the people involved unless it's relevant to the story. I will, however, mention race when it's relevant. Suffice it to say that most of my stories take place in communities with a large black population. This is the demographic structure of Oakland. Consequently, many of the people I dealt with as victims of crimes and suspects of crimes were black. I use the terms race and black or white reluctantly, but these are terms we understand today. So far as I am concerned, God only created one race, the human race. Unfortunately, people divide themselves and others into what they call races on the basis of language, skin color and various physical characteristics. Wouldn't it be nice if we could get beyond superficial differences?

I deeply resented being assumed by many people to be racist because I was white and a police officer. Before I became a police officer, I suspected that many white police officers were racist as this was the impression I got from news sources. Once I was wearing the blue, I found this to be a false generalization. I came to realize there were and are white people and white police officers who are racist, but it was not tolerated on the Oakland Police Department. I also knew that it was racist for people to assume I was racist because I was white and/or a police officer. Racism is a weakness among some individuals in all races and unique to none. In some cases, there is a reason for racism but there is no justification for it.

I recognized that there was an element of hazard in my chosen career, but I was willing to face it because I believed that I was doing something important. I was in danger of being drafted into the Viet Nam war where I might lose my life in a foreign rice paddy for a dubious cause. I was much more willing to put my life on the line for something I believed in and where I felt I could make a positive contribution. I had gone through a physical examination at the Oakland Draft Board induction center and had been classified 1A. The 1A classification meant I could be drafted any day and I was hoping not to be drafted. The City of Oakland had written a letter to my local draft board requesting I be deferred from the draft to keep on as a police officer. I doubt that that made any difference but, at that same time, Valerie became pregnant and when I notified my draft board of that I was reclassified and was not likely to be drafted.

Not long after I had my military draft examination there was a major demonstration against the military draft nation-wide. The "Stop The Draft" movement in 1967 included radical and leftist elements as well as many people who didn't support the Viet Nam war and/or the idea of a compulsory draft. Locally in Oakland, thousands of demonstrators descended on the Draft Board and police were required to clear people away from the entrance of the facility so it could continue its business. Regular work hours were changed to 12-hour shifts and I was "lucky" enough to work from midnight until 12:00 noon. It was tough. On my days off I reported to a large parking facility in riot gear (helmet, long baton and gas mask on my belt) where I spent most of my time sitting around waiting for deployment. I was occasionally deployed with a squad to block off a particular street here or there. Some people jeered us, others smiled and waved and a hippie wearing a red cross emblem and carrying medical supplies offered to help any injured officers. I was not involved in any direct confrontations with the crowd where we had to push them back to clear a street. Most of this was done while I was working 12-hour shifts on my beats. By the time I was involved, we were just holding our positions.

While one gets used to the element of hazard on the job, I must confess that as a rookie officer I sometimes experienced a bit of apprehension before leaving the house for work when I was working dogwatch. I would feel this apprehension in the quiet dark of the night before leaving the house for night shift. Everyone else was asleep and I would sit and listen to quiet music on the radio as I prepared mentally to leave the comfort and warmth of the house to confront the cold dark dank night air and often hostile streets of the City.

If I left the house at 11:00 p.m., I could be at work in uniform and ready for lineup at midnight. My apprehension would always vanish by the time I arrived at work. I didn't feel this apprehension working any other shift. I think it had something to do with leaving the house in the dark of night to work in the dark. Once on the job I wasn't apprehensive - I was super alert but not apprehensive. A working police officer tends to be hyper-vigilant. First of all, you are wearing a uniform and carrying a gun and you know people tend to notice you. I was always a bit self-conscious in uniform. On top of being watched by the public you are always alert for hazards or criminal activity in your environment. You are watching traffic for violations or hazards; you are watching people for suspicious activity. If you are eating in a restaurant you usually find a place to sit with your back to a wall. You are being paid to look for trouble and you tend not to let your guard down while on duty. Being hyper-vigilant isn't a bad thing when you are on duty but perhaps not so much on your off time. I sometimes found myself in hyper- vigilant mode on my days off. Hyper-vigilance is difficult to turn off and it can impact family relationships.

Hyper-vigilance tends to help keep you safe when on duty but it's not enough. You can't be aware of everything around you and there is always the unknown hazard. If you make what you think is a routine car stop for speeding, you wouldn't know that the driver was speeding because he just robbed a bank or killed someone. He knows you are a cop, but you don't know who he is or what he just did. I was reminded of unknown hazards one night when working swing shift with another officer.

There was a 24-hour café on San Pablo Avenue in west Oakland where West street branches off to the north. Sycamore street branched off San Pablo toward the east behind a little café which was on a small island between the streets. The café was police friendly and usually left the back door open on the Sycamore street side. We would often stop behind the café on Sycamore street and step inside to get a cup of coffee in the back room. On this particular night, we were dispatched to a 415C at the café at Sycamore and San Pablo. A 415C was the code for an unknown disturbance and dispatch told us only that the cook (it was a one-man operation) told a customer to call the police. To our good fortune, we were positioned to respond to the call from the south and stopped on the San Pablo side to enter the café through the front door. When the cook saw us before we entered, he beckoned to us frantically to go around to the back. When we stepped to the back, the cook ran out the back door where we normally entered and pointed to a man running toward a car parked across West street on Sycamore. He was shouting, "There he goes....get em!" We asked, "Get who, what did he do?" The frantic cook then added, "That's him, he's got a shotgun and was trying to hold me up." At this time the car the man got into peeled out and sped into the dark eastbound on Sycamore toward Grove. As we put things together, we found out that a guy with a shotgun came in the open back door off Sycamore street and was trying to hold up the café. The cook, who was the only person running the restaurant, stalled the robber with the shotgun saying he was serving customers. He whispered to a customer, "Call the police." The customer stepped to a pay phone and called the police not knowing what the problem was and that's how we got the call. We hurried to our car in hopes of pursuing the suspect vehicle, but it was long out of sight.

This was a sobering reminder that there are always unknown hazards when on duty. If my partner and I had been in position and responded to this "unknown disturbance" from north on San Pablo or West Street, we would have parked on Sycamore street and walked in through the café's open back door, into the man with a shotgun. We would not have had our guns out so that would not likely have ended well for us.

I never had to use my gun during my law enforcement career. In Oakland, I probably had it out and pointed at someone once a week, but I never had to shoot someone. I almost shot someone once in a very close call. Another officer and I were dispatched to an armed robbery at a bar just before the 2:00 a.m. closing time. We were not far away and arrived within a minute and got a good description of the armed robber who had run around a corner just before we arrived. I drove around the corner and saw nobody on the street but, just around the corner was an abandoned two-story commercial building with a vacant restaurant on the ground floor. I noticed a ladder leading to the roof and thought perhaps the suspect had gone up to the roof to hide since I saw nobody on the street. I went up the ladder to the roof and found nobody but discovered an unlocked door to a stairway leading down inside the building which was pitch dark. With flashlight in my left hand, extended to my left side and drawn gun in my right hand I started to work my way down the stairs which had a number of turns in it. As I came around a corner, I suddenly saw a man in front of me with a gun in his hand. I started to squeeze the trigger on my gun but stopped just in time. The man with the gun in front of me was me. For some reason there was a full-length mirror on the wall in the narrow stairway. Talk about a close call, if I had discharged my gun there would have been two pounds of paperwork to complete, a discharge of firearm hearing and a lifetime of ribbing.

One quiet Sunday during day shift I was patrolling a back street on beat 8 when I came upon the scene of a vehicle accident that occurred seconds before I arrived. I saw a car partially crashed into a garage attached to a house. The car's engine was racing, and the rear wheels were spinning on a sidewalk and smoking heavily as if about to burst into flame. I went to the driver's window and found a lady who was dazed and unable to respond when I told her to turn off the engine. I reached into the car and turned off the engine and a lady in the passenger seat handed me a baby. The baby's head was distorted from the impact of the collision and he was gasping. I ran with the baby to my car and radioed for an ambulance, the fire department and another officer. I held the baby until I was able to give him to the ambulance that responded. A drunk driver had run a stop sign and struck the car with two ladies and the baby causing it to swerve into the garage with the engine racing. The baby died and this incident was added to my list of events I am unable to forget.

In 1967 when I was in my second year on the Department one of my recruit school classmates was killed and another officer seriously wounded when they made a car stop on one of the founders of the Black Panther Party. The killer had escaped but was wounded in the gunfire exchange and was arrested when he went to a hospital. This was the first of several funerals I would attend for my fellow officers during my career on OPD.

The Black Panther who killed my classmate and wounded another officer was eventually convicted of voluntary manslaughter. He served less than two years before being released on appeal based on a technicality involving jury instructions. Later he was accused of killing a juvenile prostitute and pistol-whipping a man but fled to Cuba for asylum rather than face trial. He eventually returned to the US and his trials for both killings resulted in hung juries. This was very disheartening for myself and my fellow officers on the department.

During the second trial for the murder of the officer who was my classmate, the city was tense. With a conviction there would likely be some violence or protest activity. Accordingly, we were doubled up and worked with two officers per car as much as possible. It was July and I was working dogwatch with another officer of like temperament. While the trial went on for a few days, the streets were relatively quiet. We were expecting trouble with a guilty verdict but there was no unusual activity on the street during the trial.

My partner and I were assigned to beat four, largely low-income minority in character. There was a second two-man car assigned to the beat and we noticed that after three or four in the morning they were awfully quiet. We didn't hear them on the radio, and we didn't see them patrolling the beat. Then, one night in the wee hours of the morning we saw their car parked in a darkened vacant lot under the freeway. It was backed up as far as it could go against a support structure and the lights were out. These guys were catching some Z's while we were still on the job. My partner and I were boy scouts by temperament and wouldn't think of doing anything like that, but we had a better idea. We knew there was a dead-end access road that paralleled the freeway to a point adjacent to where these guys were sleeping on the job. When we checked out our car before going on duty, we had noticed a bunch of firecrackers in the trunk. It was July and officers often just confiscate fireworks rather than arrest or cite violators. Hmmm, we thought, sleeping beat partners and fireworks, we have to do this.

Bear in mind, this is during a time when being ambushed was a concern for police officers. With this in mind we backed down the dead-end street adjacent to the sleeping/resting officers under the freeway. We got the string of firecrackers out of the trunk, lit it and threw it over the chain-link fence toward the car where the officers were resting. When it started rapidly popping, we peeled out and split the scene. The police radio remained silent, so we didn't know what kind of reaction we got from our prank. We noticed that the officers we pulled the prank on requested to meet with a couple other units in the area but never requested to meet with us. The next night we learned that we had really caught them napping. They had removed their gun belts to be comfortable and we had scared the heck out of them, they thought they were under attack. They never suspected my partner and me because we were boy scouts; they thought we would never do a thing like that. This was too good of a reaction to not claim credit for, so we confessed. They weren't entirely happy with us, but we remained friends.

In subsequent years, the Black Panther founder who had killed my recruit school classmate was arrested a few times on weapons charges and pled no contest to a charge of embezzling public funds. He was also using cocaine and was eventually shot dead by a member of The Black Guerrilla Family, a Marxist-Leninist narcotics prison gang. This seemed to affirm my belief that, one way or another, justice is absolute in the long run.

The Black Panther Party was a Marxist revolutionary group and was active in Oakland for a number of years and seemed to have a lot of public support. They organized some philanthropic endeavors in poor minority communities and sold copies of a small red book titled, "Quotations From Chairman Mao" to earn money. While the Panthers gained support from much of the community, the police department received complaints from black businesses who were being extorted for funds to support Panther causes.

The Panthers would often show up fully armed on a scene where police were conducting an investigation. This resulted in some tense situations. They wouldn't normally point their loaded rifles at a police officer which would be a violation, but they would "inadvertently" swing the barrel of a gun past an officer. They carried this practice a bit too far when they walked into the State Legislature brandishing loaded guns. This resulted in legislation prohibiting carrying a loaded firearm in public place under certain circumstances. In one sense, as a second amendment advocate, I regret this law, but it made our job safer.

The Black Panthers published and distributed a newspaper which was filled with their anti-police propaganda and portrayed the police as pigs. It was common for people to call the police pigs during that era. How ironic it was that we had an officer with the last name of "Pigg" and another with a last name of "Piggee." When on patrol I would often wave or stop to chat when I saw a youngster on the street. It was common for youngsters to say politely, "Hi Mr. Pig" when I greeted them. They didn't mean it in a derogatory way, they had just learned that police are called pigs.

On April 6th, 1968, during my third year on the Oakland Policed Department, I was working third watch (swing shift) on my north Oakland beat 8 with a second officer in the car with me. Martin Luther King Jr. had been cruelly assassinated in Memphis Tennessee two days before and there were scattered incidents of vandalism and unrest around the city, so most cars were doubled up for safety. It was a little after 9:00 p.m. and dark when we heard an officer come on the police radio with an excited voice giving his location on Union Street and calling for help and stating they were under attack. We could hear gunfire in the background on the radio as the officer was calling for help. I recall the officer calling for help and stating his partner was hit. Actually, both officers were wounded. The officers were driving on Union street when they saw someone duck down behind one of four cars parked at the curb. They stopped the police car in the street behind the parked cars and as they got out of the patrol car to investigate, they came under fire from both sides of the street. All of the shooters turned out to be Black Panthers who had been out to ambush the police. (More on this later.) One of the officers got off a few shots and managed to hit one of the suspects. Other officers responding code 3 (red lights and sirens) arrived and the suspects fled into the yards and down the street.

My partner and I responded to the area from about a mile away on beat 8. As I approached about a half block from the area of the shooting, some black residents ran out of their house, waved me down and said there were black men in their house with guns. I went to the partially opened front door of the house, racked a round into the chamber of my shotgun, which I appropriated from the car, and announced something to the effect of, "This is the Oakland Police, throw your weapons out and come out with your hands up or we'll come in shooting." I know, this sounds really stupid now, but in my defense, I used to really like western movies. In any event, as stupid as it may have been, it had the effect I was hoping for as a loaded automatic pistol flew out the door and landed at my feet. It was followed by a young black youth (he turned out to be 17 years old) with his hands in the air. He had socks tied to his belt filled with extra ammunition. I handcuffed the lad and gave him and his gun to my partner who put him into the back of the police car. I proceeded to quickly walk through each room of the house with my gun at the ready but saw nobody so I exited and told my partner I was going around the corner where the shooting started, and we could still hear some shooting. One of the black residents gathered at the scene told me, "I hope you get all the bastards." God apparently looks after stupid rookies as when other officers arrived and searched the house more thoroughly, they took two more suspects out of the house, one from under a bed and another from a closet.

When I arrived at the scene where the shooting started there was no shooting going on in that area, but I could see the police car full of holes and an ambulance was taking care of the wounded officers. Their police car was riddled with bullet holes, the count came to 49. There were a number of officers on the scene and some suspects in custody. A sergeant on the scene sent me with my shotgun into an abandoned heavily burned house adjacent to the scene with a second-floor window overlooking the area. He told me to cover the area while officers were working below. I was up there overlooking the area for some time and while there my emotions started to catch up with my actions. I was thinking how vulnerable we were as police officers. I could see lights on in nearby houses and people looking out windows. Were they residents or suspects? How could I know who the good people were and who the bad people were?

For some time, there continued to be shooting down the street and around the corner as two of the Panthers were holed up in a basement and exchanging fire with the police. Eventually the police shot teargas rounds into the house and one of the burning projectiles set the house on fire and the suspects came out from their hiding place. One suspect surrendered and complied with police commands and the other ran and refused to comply with police orders and was shot and killed.

It was an eventful night, but I learned a few days later that I was luckier that night than I ever could have imagined. It was learned through investigative interviews that the Panthers were out that night looking to ambush some police officers. Of course, my partner and I on beat 8 were unaware of this and were handling routine matters. In the course of duty, we encountered a juvenile on a stolen bicycle. We drove the youth to his home to talk to his parents and issue a juvenile citation for the probation department to follow up at some future date. It was all routine, we parked our car in the street walked across the street with the youth, did our business which just took a few minutes, then walked back to our car and drove away. What we didn't know was that the Black Panthers, looking to ambush police that night had parked their car near ours and a second car of Black Panthers were going around the block to park in a position to catch us in a crossfire when we returned to our car. While the second car was making the block to take up its position, my partner and I came out of the house, got in our car and drove away. We were completely unaware that we were being setup for an ambush.

It was admittedly sometimes difficult to keep a good attitude on the job. Some people disliked me because I was a police officer. Some people disliked me because I was white, and some disliked me because I was a white police officer. I was frequently called, "pig," "honkey," "cracker" or other colorful names while on the job. It was common for someone to spit in my direction when I drove by in my police car. This definitely dampened the idealism I came on the job with.

I was feeling a lot of stress on the job during these years, and I don't think I was an exception. It seemed we were under attack in the media and on the street and the "system" wasn't taking it seriously. Stress can manifest in many ways. Loud noises on or off duty were particularly bothersome to me. I know my stress impacted my relationship with my wife and daughter. With stress added to hyper-vigilance, I probably wasn't the husband I should have been. I was blessed with an understanding wife.

One night two officers working in north Oakland set the example for how not to handle stress. In the wee hours of the morning, they got drunk on duty and shot up the Black Panther headquarters, driving around the block at least twice to shoot the windows out. Of course, they were arrested and fired but I felt shame for weeks. Not only did they get drunk on duty, but in shooting up the Black Panther headquarters they appeared to affirm all the lies the Panthers were claiming about police conduct. I was white and wearing the same blue uniform these officers did and I felt deep shame. When a fellow officer was attacked or killed, I felt I was also attacked. Now, when officers acted shamefully, I felt the shame.

Race was and continues to be an issue in law enforcement. I saw myself as protecting the public, trying to reduce crime, taking bad guys off the street so good people could live in peace. Every day I was taking reports from black people who were the victim of crimes, yet when detaining or arresting black suspects I was seen as racist and oppressive. I thought I was here to help, I thought I was helping. I came to realize that most people I had contact with, whether the victim or perpetrator of a crime, were not having a good day and I wouldn't necessarily be seen as one of the good guys.

I had a particularly bad day working swing shift on beat 8 on a hot summer night. A couple other officers and I were dispatched to what was described as a street fight. On arrival there were a number of people in the street arguing and it turned out it all started over a couple of juveniles who were in a fight. One of the juveniles had obtained a butcher knife and took a swing at the other juvenile cutting his shirt but only leaving a scratch across his stomach with minimal bleeding. This seemed a straightforward assault with a deadly weapon. We got names and stories, took custody of the knife and the youth who tried to stab the other boy. We intended to deliver him to Juvenile for processing. In the meantime, the crowd had grown a little larger and wasn't particularly friendly, so we decided to place the arrestee in a car and change locations to do our paperwork to avoid allowing things to escalate where we were. One of the officers put the arrestee in the back of his police car but when he tried to close the door a man stopped him and began to struggle with the officer.

At this point, I needed to take action, but I wasn't too smart about it. He was wrestling with the officer in front of the open back door of the police car so I decided that rather than trying to wrestle with him from behind I would use my police baton on his shoulder to immobilize his arm first. Our standard gear included what we called a short baton about 12 inches long made of hard plastic. It fit into a special pocket in the back of our uniform pants. In other days it might have been called a billy club but we called it a baton. In the training we received about using the baton we were told to NEVER hit someone on the head with it. If we had to use it, we were instructed to strike the bony tip of the shoulder which would temporarily immobilize the arm so we could gain control. I was behind him so I had a good shot at the subject's head, but I was told to never hit the head. All of this reasoning happened in a couple seconds but I decided to pass up the head and strike him hard on the top of his shoulder to temporarily immobilize that arm… just like it said in the training manual and as we were told in training. I delivered what I judged to be a considerable whack on his left shoulder and immediately found the training manual was wrong. Not only did it not immobilize his arm, it pissed him off. As soon as I delivered the blow, I was grabbed from behind by someone much stronger than I was. The pissed off fellow I had hit on the shoulder turned around and easily wrenched my baton from my hand and proceeded to whack me on the head with it. He apparently had not read the training manual. I was grabbed from behind over the shoulder and had limited movement of my arms, but I managed to lift my left arm up to deflect the next blow to the head which came down on my left wrist and smashed my wristwatch which stopped it at 8:07 p.m. I still have this smashed watch as a souvenir (see back cover).

Things got pretty fuzzy for me, but I was pulled backwards and started to fall and managed to turn around to land face down with someone sitting on top of me. My arms were pinned but I could hold my face off the sidewalk. I was surrounded by people and I saw a juvenile was about to deliver a kick to my face, so I managed to turn my head and took the hit on the back of the head. The kid went around to the other side and again tried to kick me in the face and I again managed to turn my head it time to take the kick to the back of the head.

During this time, other officers were having their own difficulties but one managed to get to his radio and broadcast a "940B." The 940B code means an officer is in trouble and needs help. The 940B code isn't used for routine calls for assistance so when it is broadcast, it gets an immediate response. I don't know how long I was down being pummeled but I do recall hearing sirens and a streak of blue passing over my back when another officer was taking someone off my back. People were running everywhere as help arrived and soon, I found I could get up on my hands and knees. Beneath me, I had been lying on it, was my revolver. It had come out of my holster and ended up under me. It would have been most unfortunate if someone had been able to get their hands on it when I was incapacitated. I am convinced that the Lord protected me on a number of occasions. I was dazed and when I got to my feet, I saw a black cloud closing around my field of vision as I started to pass out. I had experienced this once before in college when I bounced out of control off a trampoline and landed on the hardwood floor of the gymnasium. I didn't completely pass out on either occasion, but the encroaching black cloud stuck as a memory. On this occasion I leaned against a nearby police car until my head quit spinning and my vision cleared up. I found my baton on the sidewalk nearby, so I managed to make it with no loss of equipment and with a few lumps and bruises but no major injuries.

I didn't know it at the time but the juvenile who kicked me in the head was identified and arrested and the adult who hit me with my baton was identified and later arrested. I went to juvenile court for the kid that kicked me in the head and listened to his attorney describe how his client was caught up in the moment and had no ill toward me as he was kicking me in the head. The juvenile was soon released. The adult who fought with us and hit me on the head with my baton was allowed to plead guilty to misdemeanor resisting arrest. I struggled with my attitude for some time after this incident.

I have mentioned previously that a cynic is an idealist turned inside out. I think this is a good working description of a cynic. I have to admit that it was very difficult during these days to avoid turning cynical. Many of us entering into a career in law enforcement are, to some extent, idealists. We think we will be the good guys and we will catch the bad guys and we will make life better for the other good guys. The reality an officer encounters on the street and in the justice system itself can be a brick wall that turns an idealist into a cynic when they hit it. It seemed to me that somewhere around the third year on the job, a certain number of officers find this isn't a good career path for them. Ideally, if they can't work through the cynicism, they find another job. Unfortunately, some turn cynical but stay on the job to be a supervisor's nightmare. Others retire but fail to notify management, they stay on the job with minimal productivity or incentive. They are happy to take a report after a crime is committed but are not inclined to seriously pursue suspects or hurry to the next call. They plod through the day, take their time and, to the extent possible, avoid situations with risk.

While still in recruit academy, I encountered a fellow in the basement locker room emptying his locker. He told us he had just quit. I asked him why and all he would say was, "You just get tired of the "bullshit." One person's "bullshit" is another person's career. It's not a job for everyone.

CHAPTER 8

FROM OPD TO FBI TO OPD

After working the street for a few years, I decided I would like to try something different so, in 1969, I applied for a transfer to the Planning and Research Division. I have always appreciated my ability to work in a variety of assignments on OPD. The assignments were so diverse that it was almost like having several different careers in one. In order to be considered for an assignment to the Planning and Research Division, I was interviewed by the Division Commander and required to do a study on my own time and submit a research paper. I obtained a stack of raw data having to do with the number and types of calls for service by hour of the day and submitted an analysis which I titled something like "One Man – Two Man Car Study." Of course, today it would be titled "One Person – Two Person Car Study" but the idea was to determine whether deploying one-man or two-man police units was more effective. The effective deployment of limited personnel resources as well as officer safety were factors to be considered. I don't remember all the results of my study except that it was clear that two-person police units were justified during certain hours and in certain areas.

Only one officer needs to be dispatched to take a report but two units or a two-person unit would be sent to crimes in progress and various disturbances where there was a known or potential element of hazard. Two units or a two-person unit was always sent to family disturbance where things could go wrong quickly. I learned this as a rookie with my first training officer when we were greeted at the door by a man waving a hammer in a threatening manner.

I don't think my "One Man – Two Man Car Study" revealed anything everyone didn't already know intuitively, but it passed muster and I was loaned from Patrol Division to the Planning and Research Division. While in Planning and Research, I wore a suit and tie to work rather than a uniform and worked on a number of projects having to do with report flow through the Department, data and information collection and distribution and such. We were in an age when digital data was limited compared to today. We didn't have the ability to fully digitize police reports in those days, so microfilm and microfilm access technology was something I was looking at. While in Planning and Research I also assisted on a project to obtain a federal grant that allowed OPD to start a helicopter program.

I have always been interested in helicopters and while I am admittedly a bit of a white-knuckle flyer, I was happy to go on a flight in a Bell Jet Ranger helicopter as part of my participation and research into the grant project. As a result of the grant project, the Department did obtain a couple helicopters, but they were the Hughes 300C not the sporty Bell jet copters. As part of my interest in helicopters, I ended up with an operator's manual for the 300C and I enjoyed studying how the controls worked and even toyed with applying for the helicopter program. My interest in helicopters has persisted but I have learned from a friend who was a Navy jet pilot and my nephew who is a commercial jet pilot that there is a certain friendly rivalry, if not disdain, between fixed wing pilots and helicopter pilots. As my nephew explained it, helicopters don't fly like a proper aircraft. They merely beat the air into submission.

During this time, I had been in communication with one of my recruit academy classmates who had left OPD to join the FBI. I was not dissatisfied with OPD or my career path there, but I found that with a college degree and three years of municipal law enforcement experience, I was qualified to apply to the FBI. At the time I thought of the FBI as the ultimate law enforcement agency and began to think of it as a logical career path. After discussing it with my wife, I applied to the FBI, took the various tests and a physical exam.

In February of 1970 I received a letter signed by Director John Edgar Hoover offering me the position of Special Agent with the Federal Bureau of

Investigation. If I were to accept the position, I was to report to Washington D.C. on May 4th. This was exciting but it meant for some big changes in our lives. I accepted the appointment and notified my boss, the commander of Planning and Research, that I would be resigning to join the FBI in a couple months. The commander tried to tempt me to stay with OPD by offering to allow me the opportunity to train as a helicopter pilot. He was aware of my fascination with helicopters. While his offer was mildly tempting, I saw it as a dead-end career path, especially when compared to the FBI.

On April 17th, I resigned from OPD to accept a position with the FBI. Since I had no idea where I would be assigned with the FBI, we sold our house in Livermore and put all our belongings except what we would need for travel into storage. We loaded our Volkswagen bug and set off for Washington D.C. The trip took six days, and it was a bit rugged with a loaded bug, the two of us and a two year old child. Val had planned it well and each day she presented our daughter with a new toy to keep her occupied during the long hours of driving. She had arranged a bed on top of our luggage in the back seat and our daughter slept a lot during the day. This was a bit problematic as when we found a motel after a hard day of driving our daughter was not sleepy and was full of energy. We desperately needed rest, but the daughter was ricocheting off the walls with unbounded energy.

When we arrived in Washington D.C. it was hot with the usual stifling East Coast humidity. I went into FBI headquarters and got some recommended apartment locations and we set out to find a place to stay while in FBI training. We found an unfurnished apartment in nearby Landover Maryland, rented minimal furniture and settled in. I was to report in on May 4th which was our daughter's 3rd birthday. We had a few days to wait so we celebrated Kathy's birthday a few days early. At night, I ran with her, chasing fireflies, which we had never seen before.

On May 4th I reported to what the FBI called New Agent's Class number 16 or NAC 16 in downtown Washington D.C. The FBI didn't have a dedicated office building in those days but had offices in the Old Post Office Building and the nearby Department of Justice building. Most of our classes were in the Old Post Office Building. The first thing that happened on reporting in was that we were all fingerprinted to make sure we were who we said we were.

The FBI's NAC 16 was a little intense as one would expect but it didn't have the para-military flavor that the police academy had. We had classes on FBI reporting and investigative procedures, federal law and procedures, physical training and all the stuff one would expect. We were given four fat manuals full of rules and regulations which made it clear that I couldn't eat breakfast on my day off without violating some rule somewhere. Rules even specified what you could have on top of your desk at work.

We spent a couple weeks on a Marine base in Virginia where we had extensive firearms training. I enjoyed that and got to shoot pistols, rifles, and a Thompson machine gun. The FBI did have some excellent firearms instructors and one day they gave us a demonstration that was interesting. From a distance, an agent shot the tip of an ax blade that split the bullet in two popping balloons on either side behind the ax. He also accurately shot a target behind him by looking at a reflection in his diamond ring. I didn't know it before, but if you hold a diamond near your eye and to the side and rotate it you will see a reflection of what is behind you. He used that reflection to hit the target.

It was hot and terribly humid on the base but that was typical East Coast weather. Often during the training there were significant thunder and lightning storms, day or night, with pouring rain. I became friends with one of the agents in the class who was from Louisiana. He and his wife and family stayed in the same apartment complex we were in in Landover, Maryland. He was a helicopter pilot in Viet Nam and had become one of the pilots that flew Marine 1 which was the helicopter that flew the president or vice president. Marine 1 was housed on the Marine base where we were so we got to tour it. It was heavily guarded but we were FBI agents (ta da) so we got to tour it up close and personal. I loved helicopters so I particularly enjoyed the opportunity. It was well polished as one would expect and outfitted with luxurious leather seats.

After weapons training in Virginia, we returned to Washington D.C. for more classroom training and we spent a week working with fellow agents in the Washington D.C. field office. While working with field agents we arrested a juvenile who had robbed a bank at gunpoint but managed to leave a palmprint on the teller's counter during the robbery. He was released from custody while we were still working on the paperwork. Somehow that seemed familiar.

One day during our training in Washington D.C. we were sent to a nearby auditorium to fill some seats while J. Edgar Hoover addressed the graduation of a National Academy of law enforcement officials. The FBI puts on training programs for law enforcement people sent from departments around the country. The National Academy is one such program. This was the only time we saw Mr. Hoover during our training.

So, now that I was seeing the FBI from the inside, how did it stand up to the reputation or high expectations that I had? To be sure, the FBI had a lot of fine, highly skilled and dedicated agents but I found myself getting disillusioned. On the walls around the offices in Washington D.C. there were photos of gangsters from the 20's and 30's, the years when J. Edgar Hoover made his mark and came to fame. I wasn't impressed by such nostalgia, I was thinking, "That was then, this is now."

We learned that, in the past, every agent in the new agent training program would be sent to meet and shake hands with Mr. Hoover in his office. However, Mr. Hoover would fire any agent he determined to have a sweaty palm. He claimed you can't trust anyone with a sweaty palm. During my class we were sent to greet one of the Assistant Directors rather than Mr. Hoover and we were instructed to run our hand down our pant leg before shaking hands to make sure we didn't have a sweaty palm. Really!? We heard stories of agents being transferred or demoted for embarrassing the Bureau. Some out of the way assignments were considered bone yards for agents that embarrassed the Bureau. I remember hearing that you don't want to screw up and end up in Butte Montana. At the time that didn't sound like a bad assignment to me.

During my week working with field agents, I heard some say they would quit tomorrow if they had another job to go to. Morale wasn't what I expected. I was taken by Mr. Hoover's house and the agent told me this story. One day Mr. Hoover found some poop on his back patio. Rather than throw it in the garbage he called for an agent to come and pick it up and find out what it was. It was sent to the FBI lab and the answer was determined to be raccoon poop. The agent informed Mr. Hoover and thought that would be the end of it but, it wasn't. Mr. Hoover told the agent, "Find it." The agent was no fool and managed to find a raccoon in an animal facility. He acquired the animal and donated it to a local zoo. The agent informed Mr. Hoover that the raccoon had been located and donated to a local zoo in his name. That closed the mysterious case of poop on the patio.

During my time in training with the FBI a number of disappointments and concerns began to accumulate. I didn't see the Bureau from the inside the way it had looked from the outside. I had not left OPD because I was dissatisfied with it but because I felt I was going to an elite federal agency. When I encountered people who learned that I was an FBI agent they were impressed, but I wasn't. I felt more pride as a police officer in Oakland. I felt I did more real police work in a week than I would as an FBI agent in a month or more. I also learned that I would be sent to my first field office for a year then transferred somewhere else. All this moving around in a job that was losing its appeal made me begin to wonder if I had made a mistake. I considered resigning while still in the training program but decided that would look like I had flunked out or failed. I decided to see it through to my first field office. Perhaps things would be better outside of Washington D.C.

As my 14 weeks of training in the FBI's NAC 16 drew to a close, I received notice that my first field office assignment would be San Antonio, Texas. In accordance with FBI policy, I had to submit a letter with my travel itinerary listing each motel where I would stay when traveling from Washington D.C. to San Antonio. This was in the days before cell phones, and we had to be reachable at all times. The trip from Washington D.C. to San Antonio was uneventful, I've already mentioned the oppressive humidity on the East Coast and now I can report that it extends into the south. It was late August so the heat, even without the humidity, would be memorable.

By the time we arrived in San Antonio and found a motel to stay in I was seriously thinking about returning to OPD. I had a few days before I had to report so we spent some time with a realtor looking for a place to rent. I liked San Antonio and we had a nice dinner on the River Walk downtown near the Alamo. The town and people were friendly, but my insides were churning. The next day, I called OPD Personnel Division and asked what the possibility was of returning to OPD. I was told, we'll call you back. A short time later, I got a call informing me that the Chief of Police says, "welcome back."

On August 19th, I reported to the San Antonio FBI office and submitted my resignation. We were on the road heading back to Oakland within an hour. It had been a wild ride and Valerie stuck with me through it all. I felt bad about leaving the FBI after their training investment in me but inside I knew that municipal law enforcement, in Oakland in particular was my career choice. I felt more pride as an officer on the streets of Oakland than as an FBI agent anywhere. While I was disillusioned by my FBI experience, I don't intend to reflect negatively on the Bureau. On the whole it's a great organization with many fine personnel doing good work. The FBI has it's 10% of flakes just like OPD or any other outfit but it isn't reflected in their reputation. It just wasn't for me. Like I said at the end of chapter seven, one man's bullshit is another man's career.

On September 8th, 1970 I was reinstated to the Oakland Police Department and assigned to work in the jail to fill a vacancy where they were short of jailers. Jailers are civilian personnel, that is, they are not sworn peace officers. On occasions when they are short a jailer an officer would sometimes be assigned to fill in. I was assigned to the jail for almost two months, but I didn't mind. I was home and it felt like it.

After returning to Oakland, Valerie and I decided to look for a home closer than Livermore where we had our first home. Livermore was a great town, but the commute was excessive. We found an affordable older home in Castro Valley which provided for a much easier commute.

After my time working the jail I was assigned to Patrol where I worked for a short while before being loaned to Research and Development Division which was the old Planning and Research Division with a different name. Photography was a hobby for me and while working in Research and Development I was assigned to take photographs of the OPD helicopter operation for an article the division commander was writing for the FBI Bulletin. The "FBI Law Enforcement Bulletin" is a monthly magazine that is distributed to law enforcement agencies world-wide. I enjoyed photographing the helicopter unit and got to fly with them in the process. One of my photographs was the cover photo on the July 1971 FBI Law Enforcement bulletin. In 1972 the article with my pictures was published in the "Bulletin" the magazine of the British South African Police. Apart from the photo assignment I worked on various projects in Research and Development for a few months until I managed to get transferred to a great assignment in the Special Operations Section of the Preventative Services Division.

The Special Operations Section or SOS as it was called was one of my favorite assignments on OPD. Normally we worked in uniform but in unmarked cars. We patrolled the streets responding to crimes in progress and targeting high crime areas. We were not subject to taking routine calls for service like taking reports, investigating accidents, going to family fights, we were out to catch bad guys. We were deployed based on crime patterns and trends. Sometimes we worked in plain clothes to make drug or prostitution arrests.

Working in unmarked cars was advantageous as it allowed us to approach certain situations unnoticed. Of course, the practiced criminals could spot an unmarked police car from a mile away, but it still gave us a slight advantage. In this assignment we didn't write a lot of traffic tickets unless it was a particularly flagrant or dangerous violation. On one occasion I was in my unmarked card driving west on a one-way street when a car slightly in front of me in the lane to my right started to turn across my lane to go south at an intersection. I hit my brakes and blew my horn to avoid hitting him. The driver continued to make the turn, looked toward me and reached out the window and gave me the finger. At about this time he noticed that I was a cop in uniform in an unmarked car and it looked like his hand giving me the finger melted. I tapped the siren and he pulled over and was completely silent as I wrote him a ticket for making a turn from the wrong lane. I didn't lecture people when I wrote a ticket, but I would normally make sure they understood the violation. On this occasion I didn't find it necessary to explain the violation. I was professional about it, but I knew that he knew that I was exulting inside as I wrote the ticket.

On the 21st of December 1971, while working SOS, I took the sergeant's promotional exam. In January of 1972, much to my chagrin, I was loaned from SOS back to Research and Development to work on a project. In February of 1972, I took the oral exam for sergeant of police and was placed on the sergeant promotional list. On June 26, 1972, I was promoted from police officer to sergeant of police.

CHAPTER 9

SERGEANT OF POLICE

The position of Sergeant of Police on the Oakland Police Department is the first step increase in rank above police officer and is a supervisory position much of the time. Most of the investigator positions in the Criminal Investigation Division (CID) were also staffed by sergeants. I was never assigned to CID which was fine with me. In my assignments as Sergeant, I was always in a supervisory position rather than an investigative position.

As in any job where one is appointed from the ranks to a supervisory position there is a psychological transition. You are no longer one of the guys, you are a supervisor. It is necessary to keep a certain social distance from the people you supervise when on duty. You can be friendly but not a friend in the sense you were before you became a supervisor. I guess that's where the expression, "It's lonely at the top" comes from. I would never be anywhere near the top but promotion to supervisory and command positions involve a certain distancing and isolation. I still had friends in all ranks but there was a professional distancing both up and down rank when on the job.

Upon being promoted to sergeant in 1973, my first assignment was to the Communications Division. The Communications Division is sort of the nerve center of the police department. All calls for service on emergency and non-emergency phone lines came into the Communications Division and were answered by Police Communications Dispatchers. Police Communications Dispatchers were uniformed civilian personnel.

Every citizen calling the police for help starts by talking to a Police Communication's Dispatcher in the Communications Division. Police Communications Dispatchers also operated the radio system to dispatch field units to assignments as appropriate.

During any given shift, Police Communications Dispatchers would rotate through assignments involving answering incoming calls for service or operating the police radio system to dispatch field personnel. When answering the phones, they were called complaint operators and when on the radio they were referred to as dispatch operators, or more commonly, just dispatchers. The dispatch operators in the Dispatch Unit were separated from complaint operators, in the Complaint Unit, by a wall to minimize noise and distractions in the smaller Dispatch Unit where the radio operations were ongoing. During my initial assignment to the Communications Division, the complaint operators in the Complaint Unit sat on either side of a long table that had slots and a conveyor belt running from the Complaint Unit, through the wall into the Dispatch Unit. A complaint operator receiving a call for service would record the information on a specialized card and drop the card into a slot in the middle of the table where the conveyer belt carried it into the Dispatch Unit where officers were dispatched over the radio.

I refer to my initial assignment to the Communications Division as in the days BC. By that I meant Before CAD. CAD stands for Computer Assisted Dispatching and I will talk more about that later. During my initial assignment to the Communications Division, complaint operators answered the incoming phone calls and recorded information on a specialized IBM card. (If you know what an IBM card is, you probably know what a record player, clutch and running board are.) The complaint operator would obtain and record essential information about the nature of the call, the location, the name of the caller and pertinent details. The complaint operator would look up the address of the incident on a sort of vertical standing rolodex located at their position in order to determine what beat the call was on. It was necessary to know the beat so the dispatch operator would know the closest or responsible officer to send to the call. The complaint operator on the phones would also determine the priority of the call and the higher priority calls for service were recorded on cards with a red border to catch the attention of the dispatcher.

Once the complaint operator had recorded all information on the card, they would time stamp the card and drop it into one of two slots in the conveyer belt in the center of the table. The conveyer belt would quickly move the call for service card to the dispatcher for either the west sector or the east sector of the city depending on which slot the complaint operator placed the card. At the time calls for service were dispatched on one of two radio channels which were dedicated to the east or west sector. There was a third channel in the dispatch unit where a dispatcher, called the service operator, had access to telecommunications links in order to run license and warrant checks for field officers. The service operator would also order tows and other service functions for officers in the field.

This description of dispatch operations seems archaic today after the advent of computer assisted dispatching (CAD) but it was efficient and high tech compared to previous operations. Dispatchers worked in shifts similar to the Patrol Division with periodic rotations from day shift to midnights to swing shift. The division had a commander who was a lieutenant, and each shift was staffed by a sergeant supervisor and a number of civilian Police Communications Dispatchers. In later years, a civilian supervisory position, called a Senior Dispatcher, was added to the mix.

I enjoyed my first assignment as a sergeant supervisor to the Communications Division or the "radio room" as it was commonly called. I appreciated the skills required to be a dispatcher and found the Communications Division to be a key component of overall police operations. I was in a position to monitor almost everything happening in the city involving the police department. It was the one location where incoming calls for service from the public and police radio traffic to and from field personnel interfaced. In addition to supervising complaint and dispatch operations, my field experience helped me assist and coordinate with field supervisors during major incidents. My job included fielding calls from the media regarding major incidents and investigating complaints against complaint and dispatch operators from the public or police personnel.

Word must have got out that I was enjoying my assignment to Communications Division because, in just short of six months I was notified I was being transferred to the Records Division. I was highly upset because I liked working where I was and being sent to the Records Division seemed like being sent to Siberia. I asked through channels if I could appeal the transfer and was granted a meeting with the Deputy Chief of the Bureau of Services who listened politely to my plea and then proceeded to tell me how important the job was in Records and how I was uniquely qualified for the position. I could see through the smoke and mirrors and knew my appeal was fruitless, so I resigned myself to the transfer. Even so, the scratch and claw marks from the 7th floor Communications Division to the 3rd floor Records Division were visible for a number of years.

In the Communications Division, I wore a uniform, in the Records Division I wore a suit and tie. The one nice thing about the assignment was that I worked straight days and had weekends off. The assignment was every bit as exciting as you might imagine a job in the Records Division might be. The Division was managed by a Lieutenant who would be my boss. He had been my boss when I was in Planning and Research and I liked him, but I always suspect he was the reason I ended up in Records. In addition to supervising certain civilian personnel, I found myself to be the custodian of police records and would coordinate with the City Attorney's office when records were subpoenaed. I also managed towing contracts with the various towing companies the department utilized. The police department is continually ordering tows for vehicles in accidents, abandoned autos, recovered stolen cars, when the driver is arrested or when the car is evidence. I handled complaints from the department against tow companies and complaints by tow companies against the police department. After a few months in records, I submitted a letter requesting to be transferred to the Patrol Division.

After a year as a sergeant in the Records Division I was happy to be transferred to the Patrol Division and into what was one of the best assignments I had while on OPD. I was the district sergeant assigned to District 1 which included downtown and West Oakland. I appreciated the diversity of the district as it ranged from downtown commercial to low income residential. It also included the Oakland estuary and Port of Oakland facilities. I was working rotating shifts again with midweek days off, but I was in uniform and on the line and that suited me fine. I would be supervising officers assigned to beats 1 through 7 as well as two officers assigned to a paddy wagon and an evidence technician.

Apart from the nature of the work, supervision of police officers is probably like any typical supervisory position. One tends to spend the bulk of their supervisory energies on a small percentage of people being supervised. It seems every supervisor has a few problem children. While I was supervising officers under me, I was under a Lieutenant of Police who was my supervisor. I always tried not to be my lieutenant's problem child, but it was always irritating when a new lieutenant or captain came on board. It seemed that just when things were running smooth, along came a new captain or lieutenant with different ideas and priorities and things would be rocky until we adjusted to the idiosyncrasies of the new command staff.

While a Patrol sergeant, I had a few different lieutenants but had the same captain most of the time. He was an ex-marine and it showed but he was older and had a mellow interior if you managed to get past the gruff exterior. I liked him as a commander as he exuded a contagious confidence, but he did have one idiosyncrasy. He was frequently on my back, either directly or through my lieutenant to make sure my officers wore their hats when outside of their police car. There was a written regulation that required officers to wear their cap when on duty outside of their police vehicle. There was some justification for the rule as the cap had a badge that reflected authority and the cap and badge easily identified an officer who might be chasing a suspect through somebody's back yard. However, this rule was disliked by many and a subject of frequent complaints. I personally had no problem with the rule. My thinking was, "This is great, all I have to do is wear this hat and do what they want me to do and I get paid well every month – no problem." I enforced the hat rule as best I could but there are occasions when an officer bails out of his car to chase a fleeing suspect and it's not practical to grab or worry about your hat first. However, If the captain rolled by a major incident where hatless officers were out of their cars dealing with suspects, I was sure to hear about it.

One day shift I was driving near the estuary and noticed one of my officer's police car parked along the road. I didn't see the officers around, it was a two-man car, so I checked and found the car was unlocked and inside on the seat were two caps. The officers were obviously on foot in the area but not chasing suspects or we would have heard them reporting on the radio. They had left the car unsecured and weren't wearing their hats, so I confiscated both hats and quickly drove away. They should have been wearing their hats and they should have locked their vehicle when away from it – I had them cold.

After a while I heard the officers back in their vehicle asking on the radio to meet up with various adjacent beat officers. They were hoping one of their fellow beat officers had swiped their hats as a prank. I was as pleased as a coyote in a hen house with my confiscated caps and was enjoying seeing or hearing them squirm as they checked around with other officers to see if anybody knew about their missing caps. I was too pleased to keep this to myself so I happened to encounter one of my officers who was never a problem and showed him the caps and explained the circumstances so he could enjoy the panic of the capless duo with me. This officer, nicknamed Red, had a better idea. He got on the police radio and announced that he had just had two male juveniles split from him and they were carrying some kind of hats, possibly a fireman's caps. Within a split second the officers with the missing hats volunteered to respond and search for the suspects. Not wanting the call to get out of hand, I waited for the capless duo to arrive and returned their caps with a warning. I had made them sweat and made my point; sometimes it's fun to be a supervisor.

In my role as a supervisor, I would, on occasion, have to discipline an officer. I didn't enjoy that part of the job but it's necessary and comes with the turf. Any disciplinary action required about four pounds of paperwork but that too was part of the job. I must have had some effect as a supervisor because I eventually made the bathroom wall of fame. There was a small restroom attached to the transportation building where we parked our police cars. One day I noticed someone had written, "Sergeant Nelson drinks here" with an arrow pointing to the urinal. Based on the timing of the matter and the level of maturity involved, I had a good idea who had done it, but I wouldn't give him the pleasure of noticing it or mentioning it.

During my time as sergeant in Patrol, heroin was the most problematic drug on the street. In future years, crack cocaine would dominate but heroin was more common at the time. Much crime on the street is associated with drug use. Addicts rob and steal to support their habit and drug dealers kill each other over turf wars. Fatal drug overdoses were common. I remember a double homicide on Christmas day in an apartment where two men were tied with hands behind their back and stabbed to death with a steak knife. There was a small quantity of heroin and user paraphernalia on the kitchen counter.

In the days leading up to Christmas there seemed to be an increase in burglaries and armed robberies. It was people doing their Christmas shoplifting early. Perhaps it was my cynicism, a persistent mild form, but the police radio broadcasting, "Any unit for a 211 (robbery) at (location)" seemed almost like hearing Jingle Bells on the A.M. radio. I had come to associate increased robberies with the holiday season.

During my patrol sergeant years, the Black Panthers were still an issue but confrontations with Black Muslims was the greater issue. If an officer stopped a car that happened to be operated by a Black Muslim, it was common for another Black Muslim car to pull in behind the officer. Routine car stops could be tense situations. Around the Bay Area law enforcement had some violent incidents involving Black Muslims. An element of the Black Muslims in the Bay Area became very violent and anti-white. This manifested itself in what came to be known as the Zebra murders. A small number of Black Muslims killed up to 70 or more white people seemingly at random. I had occasion to visit a Zebra killing scene one night where a man who was sitting in a chair watching television was killed. He was sitting in a window visible from the sidewalk and shot several time through the window which was shattered. There were bullet casings on the sidewalk outside the window.

During the time of the Zebra killings, my officers had occasion to arrest a Black Muslim and found Muslim documents in his car calling for the murder of white people which were described as "devils." A Black Muslim who kills four devils (white people) was said to earn a special button to wear on his lapel and a free trip to the Holy City Mecca (which I believe was Detroit) to see brother Mohammed. I believe that would have been Elijah Muhammad at the time.

It seems every generation has its problems. In addition to Black Panthers and Black Muslims, there were predominantly white terrorist organizations, like the Weathermen or Weather Underground and Symbionese Liberation Army (SLA) operating around the nation and the Bay Area. The Oakland Police Department was damaged when a small bomb went off in a public restroom. PG&E power line towers were blown up in the Oakland Hills and it seemed bombs were popular with a number of rag tag radical groups.

Before being promoted to sergeant, I was dispatched to check out a suspicious lunch box at the front door of a Safeway Headquarters building in Oakland. It was a Sunday, and it didn't appear the office building was occupied but I found a black lunch pail sitting there in front of the door. I knew not to move it or use my radio in the vicinity, but I put my ear to it to see if I could hear ticking and that's when I noticed a hole in the side of the lunchbox and a burnt fuse to a substantial pipe bomb inside. The fuse had gone out before it set off the bomb. I retreated some distance and radioed for the bomb squad while my guardian angel put in for a transfer. I believe this bomb targeting Safeway had to do with farm labor union issues and a boycott of table grapes. It seems there's no shortage of good reasons to blow something or somebody up.

The Symbionese Liberation Army or SLA was a leftist terrorist organization that arose and was active between 1973 and 1975. They came into wide notoriety when they kidnapped 19-year-old heiress Patricia Hearst in Berkeley. In 1973 they killed Marcus Foster, the first black school superintendent in the City of Oakland using cyanide tipped bullets. Their grievance was that they believed Foster intended to require identification cards for students in Oakland schools. For this they murdered him and seriously wounded his assistant. In reality, Foster opposed school identification cards, so their senseless murder was doubly senseless.

Two SLA members were arrested for the murder of Foster and when detained in the Alameda County Court House in downtown Oakland, they attempted to escape. I was working day shift with my crew on that date and was dispatched with several of my officers and directed to respond to the courthouse jail. On arrival, we found things well under control by Alameda County sheriff deputies, but one deputy had been savagely beaten and another had a pencil protruding from the underside of his jaw. The SLA members had been given pencils for notes when meeting with their attorney and one of them made a fist with the pencil protruding between his fingers and punched it into the underside of the deputy's jaw with an upward punch. Other deputies were able to respond and gain control to prevent the escape. Prisoners in their cells got rowdy with all the commotion and I was dispatched with some officers in the event we were needed. The deputy with the pencil protruding under his jaw wrote a phone number on a piece of paper and handed it to me with a very shaky hand. He had difficulty speaking but wanted me to call his wife to let her know he was OK. Another deputy took the number to make the call on his behalf.

As the district sergeant, I would respond to all major incidents in my district, and I liked the ability to range over a geographic area larger than a beat. As a supervisor I had no small amount of paperwork, but I didn't have to respond to take routine reports. During night hours, when calls for service were slow, I would sometimes have one or two of my officers dress in plain clothes and we would try to make arrests for prostitution or other petty street crimes. Some streets in my district were frequented by female prostitutes and/or drag queens. They were the source of frequent complaints from businesses and residents but it's difficult to make an arrest when in uniform and in a marked police car. We used plain clothes officers when we could but normally things were too busy to do this type of thing until after three or four in the morning.

San Pablo Avenue and lower 7th Street were hot spots of street crimes, drug activity and prostitution at the time. It was common for customers of the prostitutes to have their cars broken into while they were with a prostitute or they might be mugged on the street. More than once I had a prostitute's customer come up to me while pulling his pants up and ask me if I had seen a woman of a particular description run by. His story would be that she took his wallet and split when he had his pants off. I responded to one murder where an unhappy customer had returned and killed a prostitute who had taken his money and ran out on him. Street life is tough.

On lower 7th street there was a gambling shack that we were aware of. If we knocked on the door when in uniform, a slit in the door would slide open and someone would peek out. He was the raise-up-man, and he would say, "Just a minute." There would be some shuffling heard inside then the door would open, and we could walk in. There was a pool table in the center of a smoky dimly lit room. Several guys would be standing around and a couple of them might be playing pool. Against the wall opposite the pool table was a box made of half inch steel about four feet wide and five feet tall. It had a hinged door that locked from the inside and only a chair inside. There was a slot in it at about eye level and another slot lower down which could be slid open from the inside. This was the second part of their security system. They had a raise-up-man on the front door if the police were coming and someone would be inside the metal box with a gun that could be used through the lower slot if someone tried to hold up the gambling operation that would be going on at the pool table.

The gambling shack was a challenge to us. My officers working the beat wanted to see if they could bust it, but they wouldn't be able to get past the raise-up-man at the door if they were in uniform. By the time they would be let in, there would be nothing but a smoke-filled room with a bunch of men standing around a pool table. We had to actually see the gambling in progress to make any arrests. In the wee hours of dogwatch one night, we managed to get a black officer in street clothes past the raise-up-man. Once inside he saw the gambling in progress and gave a radio signal to officers standing by who moved in for the arrests. We didn't expect to shut the place down or to stop gambling in West Oakland. We met a challenge and made our point. The gambling, drug sales and prostitution would continue; we just did what we could when not tied up on more serious matters.

As an officer and later as a sergeant, I attended meetings with groups of citizens in various neighborhoods who would invariably complain about drug sales, prostitution, and street crimes as well as residential burglaries. I didn't blame them - who wants to live in a neighborhood with those ongoing activities? They seemed to think we, the police, ignored these problems, and I would explain that we did what we could with what resources we had. They would complain about streets lined with obvious prostitutes and officers just driving by without doing anything. I would explain that it's not a crime to be a prostitute, the crime is soliciting or agreeing to an act of sex for money and the prostitutes don't tend to solicit uniformed officers.

Alternatively, citizens might suggest that we allow prostitution but only in one area of the city so the rest of the city wouldn't have prostitutes standing on the corners. I never could find anyone willing to make their part of the city available for prostitution and explained that it wouldn't change anything as some prostitutes would leave the area of high competition to find a corner somewhere else in the city. These meetings were frustrating for me as a police officer but also for the citizens. They demanded and deserved an environment free of drug sales, prostitution and street crime but we could only do what we could. I would point out that usually the people we arrested for prostitution, drugs or street crime were already on probation for similar offenses. I encouraged them to make their voices heard with the district attorney and court system where these crimes are not given priority. People look to the police to make crime in their neighborhoods go away, but the criminal justice system involves more than just the police.

Arrest is not a significant deterrent where there are no significant consequences. The culture and justice system aren't willing to hand out significant consequences particularly to what they consider victimless crimes. As a police officer I felt caught in the middle of a culture and system that expected us to fix a problem that the culture and system were unwilling to fix. The police in uniform and conspicuously marked cars are seen as the system that isn't working but in reality, we are just the most visible part of the system. If the system allows a man who hit me, a uniformed police officer, on the head with my club to plead to misdemeanor resisting arrest, how serious are they going to take an arrest for prostitution, drug possession or gambling? The problem is more than a broken system; we have a broken culture, and the core of the problem is moral and spiritual.

One homicide that I encountered as a sergeant was particularly sad. Police dispatch had received a call late at night from a man who said he thought he had killed his girlfriend. He said he had hit her in the head with a heavy glass candy tray and she was unresponsive. He called again from a cell phone and said he had put her in his car and she was dead and he was driving somewhere with her. Dispatch personnel got a description of the car he was driving and his location, but he kept moving and officers couldn't locate him. When he called again, they tried to tell him to drive to the Police Department to turn himself in. I saw a car matching the description a few blocks from the Police Department and pulled it over. A woman was in the passenger seat unresponsive with an injury pattern on her forehead from the heavy dish she had been hit with. The man offered no resistance when I arrested him. I called for an ambulance, but the lady was deceased. I remember how distraught the man was for what he had done. In a moment of anger, he did something that could never be undone. Her life was ended and his was changed forever.

One of the worst assignments I had during my time as a patrol sergeant was when I was assigned with another sergeant to make arrangements for the memorial service of two fellow officers murdered in an East Oakland middle school. They had responded to a call from the school involving a man who had come on campus and was creating a disturbance. The officers located the subject and took him into a conference room where he fought with them and managed to take the gun from one officer's holster and kill them both. The suspect was subsequently captured. The other sergeant and I had to notify next of kin and meet with them to make memorial service arrangements. It was sad and sobering duty.

One very cold, dark, and foggy night one of my officers was dispatched to check out a suspicious situation at a small park on the Oakland estuary. The estuary is a body of water extending from the San Francisco Bay between the City of Oakland and the island City of Alameda. A number of marine businesses and a few restaurants border the estuary. The small park on the estuary was dimly lit and, in the fog, visibility was limited but a night watchman on a ship being repaired across an inlet from the park had observed a car pull into the park and two men were seen dragging something from the trunk of the car out on a dock walkway and throw it into the water. It looked suspicious (no kidding) so he called OPD and my officer was dispatched. I heard the call and also responded. On arrival, it was almost like a scene from a B movie. It was cold, dark, and foggy and on the narrow dock walkway which extended into the estuary some 50 feet were bloody drag marks, a pair of glasses and a little further on we saw teeth, a dental appliance of some sort in a smear of blood. At the end of the dock, was a body floating face down in the cold water. It turned out that it was a San Francisco homicide and the perpetrators had decided to dump the body in Oakland. They were ultimately identified and arrested. That scene has stuck with me because it was almost like a scene from a movie.

While being a Patrol Division district sergeant was perhaps my favorite assignment during my time on the Oakland Police Department, it was not always pleasant. The parts that weren't pleasant were just part of the job. My experiences as an officer or sergeant were not qualitatively or quantitatively different from most other officers in Oakland at the time. The job comes with the good, the bad and the ugly. It will change you; the important thing is to manage the change.

CHAPTER 10

LIEUTENANT OF POLICE

In 1977 I was promoted to the position of acting Lieutenant of Police. This was a little unusual but was the result of a political compromise. I had been scheduled to be promoted to the regular position of Lieutenant, but the Black Officer's Association objected because I was white, and they wanted a black lieutenant lower on the list to be promoted rather than me. My promotion was delayed some weeks but in the compromise that was reached, a black sergeant was promoted to the position of lieutenant and I was promoted to the position of acting lieutenant. Such is the nature of politics.

I had studied hard for the lieutenant's exam just as I had for the sergeant's exam and I was ever so pleased for the promotion. However, politics and circumstances continued to play with my head as my promotion went through some troubling cycles. Upon being promoted to acting lieutenant I was assigned to the Youth Services Division. The Youth Services Division (YSD) was the politically correct name given to what was once the Juvenile Division. In YSD I worked under a Captain and acted something like an executive officer.

The year 1978 was frustrating for me as during this year I was promoted from acting lieutenant to regular lieutenant, then because of budget issues I was demoted from lieutenant of sergeant of police then promoted from sergeant to limited duration lieutenant of police. My head was spinning in all of this. Finally, in 1979, I was promoted to regular lieutenant of police and this promotion stuck for the rest of my career. As frustrating as this was, my claim to fame was that I had been both a sergeant and lieutenant of police more often than most people in a single career.

The captain who was my boss in YSD was truly a gentleman. He ran a tight ship and I found it a little frustrating that I was on a tight leash. The captain would call me into his office from time to time and lecture me on his philosophy and how he wanted things done in the Division. He was such a gentleman that sometimes I didn't realize that during some lectures he was actually bawling me out.

My duration in YSD was uneventful with the exception of one missing juvenile case that got a lot of publicity in the press. The missing youth was later found murdered but we did a lot to find him even though we suspected he might be dead. After using blood hounds to try to find a trail I was interviewed on camera by a local TV station. This was uncomfortable for me but, in so many words I gave them the only story we could which was essentially, "The police are baffled but arrests are imminent."

Late in 1979 I was transferred from YSD to the Communications Division. I had been assigned there for a few months when promoted to sergeant, now I was going back as the commander. As a division commander, I reported directly to one of the three deputy chiefs of police rather than through a captain of police. This direct connection to the chief level was advantageous. I had much to learn, and this would end up being the longest assignment of my career on OPD. In addition to the usual supervisory and management issues I had to become knowledgeable with a number of technical systems I managed. The Communications Division had just transitioned from the previously described system where calls for service were recorded on physical cards and sent from the complaint operator to the dispatch operator by a conveyer belt. The new system was called a Computer Assisted Dispatch or CAD system. With the CAD system complaint operators wearing headsets would receive calls from the public through an automatic call distributing system (ACDS) that routed incoming calls to available complaint operators. The complaint operator was sitting at a computer terminal and would enter the information into the CAD system which would send the information to the appropriate dispatch operator. Complaint operators no longer had to manually look up the proper beat assignment for each address as the CAD system did that automatically. The CAD system was quite new on my arrival and I found I was supposed to sign off on the system so the contractors could be paid. This was awkward since I was new on the scene and didn't know CAD from cabbage. I had to talk with a lot of people using the system and involved in the implementation to feel comfortable signing off on it.

Over time I became informed and knowledgeable with the various telephone and radio systems and equipment used in the Communications Division. I worked regularly with phone company technicians and management as well as the City of Oakland radio system maintenance and engineering personnel. I learned early on that the smooth operation of the Communications Division was critical if I wanted to keep my name out of the papers. During my tenure, the 911 system was implemented, and I worked with the State director as well as phone company technicians and management on this project. Like any new system, installing it without interrupting ongoing 24-hour-a-day emergency operations was critical. Installing it was only part of the need with any new system. It was also necessary to ensure personnel were trained on the proper use of each new system so it could be successfully integrated into our operations.

Of course, 911 was a great system and it received much publicity throughout the state when it was being implemented. The 911 system would automatically direct 911 calls to the appropriate Public Safety Answering Point (PSAP). The Oakland Police Department Communications Division was the PSAP for the City of Oakland. All 911 calls for police, fire or medical emergencies came to us. 911 came with some great time and life saving features that included Automatic Number Indication (ANI) and Automatic Location Information (ALI). When a complaint operator receives a 911 call a device displays the phone number and address associated with that number.

Early on 911 demonstrated its life saving benefit as we received a call from a lady who had been kidnapped, raped, and locked into a garage. She was left alone for a few moments and found a phone in the garage where she dialed 911. She had no idea where she was but the automatic location indication feature of 911 told us where she was, and help was dispatched.

The 911 system was not without problems. The ANI/ALI information was only as good as the phone company records that provided it. There was a problem with some businesses who had phone equipment in one city that connected to a PBX (Private Branch Exchange, i.e., private phone switching system) in another city. A business in the city of Alameda might dial 911 but the call would be directed to the OPD PSAP because their PBX was located in Oakland. We had to remind dispatchers to voice verify phone number and location information.

911 was an easy way to call for police, fire or medical assistance without having to look up any emergency numbers. But it was also an easy way to get help for non-emergency situations without having to look up non-emergency numbers. Some people would use 911 to report non-urgent police matters or sometimes to ask for the non-emergency phone number. Dispatchers were instructed not to take non-emergency calls on 911 but the problem was persistent. When a limited number of emergency 911 lines are tied up on non-emergency calls, people with real emergencies may be blocked or delayed.

In spite of these problems, 911 was and is an excellent system. I was interviewed and quoted in a Newsweek magazine article that was essentially negative toward 911. I felt it gave the impression that I was negative toward the system; but I wasn't, I merely acknowledged the problems associated with it. I think 911 was hyped so much in the press that people came to think all they had to do was dial 911 and the police, fire or an ambulance would be at your door in seconds. In reality, 911 is a telephone system; it didn't give public safety more resources to respond to calls for service. It just made calls for help quicker and easier. It raised expectations that couldn't be met in the real world.

Throughout my time in the Communications Division, staffing levels and rapid response to calls for service was a problematic issue. The public expects immediate response to 911 calls but it's not always possible. If there are three telephone lines dedicated to 911 calls from a particular phone company central office and four people from that area call 911, someone is going to get a busy signal. If I had six complaint operators available answering phones and all were handling calls when someone dials 911, they would go on hold until an operator becomes available. Add to this the fact that when a major incident occurs in the public, like a shooting or serious accident, many people will dial 911 and the lines or available operators will be exceeded. If your baby isn't breathing and 911 has you on hold you can't overestimate the angst or heat generated when the story hits the press.

Add to this the heat generated by the dispatcher's union officials who hype the situation with the press to get a raise or additional dispatchers to handle the problem. I did ride the hot seat in the media from time to time because of the union's friendly association with the media. I managed to get an increase in dispatch personnel at one point but hiring and training was a slow process and always problematic. Getting the staffing levels increased was made difficult because the city had hired a company to examine the police department staffing levels and when they looked at police communications dispatcher levels they recommended against additional staffing because many calls on emergency lines were not true emergencies or multiple calls coming in may relate to a single incident. They had only looked at the situation superficially and had no concept of how the job works. Fortunately, the telephone equipment we used kept good records of the number of calls on emergency and non-emergency lines by hour of day and I was able to relate this to staffing levels to get the increase in personnel. In the end, it's not always possible to have every 911 call answered immediately.

In addition to not answering incoming calls quickly, there were also complaints about not dispatching calls quickly enough. When calls were sent from the complaint operator to the dispatch operator through the CAD system, they were given one of three priorities. A serious crime in progress would be an "A" priority, an urgent call with hazard or potential hazard involved, like an injury accident or family disturbance or prowler, would get a "B" priority and routine reports would get a "C" priority. Calls were dispatched by order of priority, not by the time the call was received. On a busy night it wasn't unusual to have 50 or more calls standing waiting for an officer to become available to handle the call. A and B priority calls would be broadcast in the blind if no officers were available. A broadcast in the blind would be, "Any unit available to handle a 211 (robbery) in progress at 1425 E.14th Street." Sometimes an officer hearing a call going out in the blind will be able to break from whatever they were handling to respond to the higher priority call. Any officer worth his or her salt won't pass up a chance to catch a criminal rather than just take a report after the fact. Often officers are dispatched from great distances, across many beats, to handle an urgent call. This is frustrating to field personnel as it draws an officer off his beat where he has primary responsibility, but it's the nature of emergency work.

While I often enjoyed the role of division commander in Communications, it was always stressful. During busy times, it was common to have many calls for service standing waiting for an officer to become available. The public didn't understand the delays and didn't appreciate it when the cause of the delay was explained. I would field citizen complains about slow response and then I would get complaints from field command personnel because we kept sending officers on calls without giving them time to do preventive patrol. If a complaint came to me directly I could usually research and explain the situation to the citizen with minimal paperwork. If the citizen complaint came from the mayor's office or chief of police, I would require an investigation and written report by the sergeant in charge of the shift where the complaint was made. If I approved the investigation, I would forward the sergeant's report to the chief of police with a cover letter and with a letter for the chief's signature to the mayor's office or the complaining citizen or both.

Some complaints involved dispatcher misconduct and discipline would be required which involved even more paperwork. I greatly admired the dispatchers as their job was very difficult. One dispatcher who had been an air traffic controller said being a police dispatcher was more difficult. Typically, half or less of all dispatchers hired would make it through the training program. Good intelligence is required for the job but more than intelligence, a certain aptitude was required. Some very bright people failed to make the grade. Given the failure rate of personnel passing the civil service test for police communications dispatcher, I worked with staff to come up with a test that tested for the aptitudes we were looking for. The new test showed promise but the city administration outside of the police department took over testing and created a single hiring list for both police and fire dispatchers which put the police department at a disadvantage. The police department had to conduct a background investigation on all hires. This delayed hiring and allowed the fire department to skim off the top of the list while we were interviewing and conducting background investigations. It was very frustrating.

To improve dispatcher training we developed a training program patterned after the police officer field training program. The program included weekly learning and performance goals which allowed us to accurately assess a trainee's progress. Still the multitasking skills required for the job put it beyond the ability of many who otherwise had the intelligence required for the job.

One of the advantages I had as commander of the Communications Division was that I was able to attend conferences put on by the Association of Public Safety Communications Officers (APCO). The APCO conferences were held at various locations around the United States and were very helpful. I was able to rub shoulders and compare notes with other people doing the same kind of work I was. These conferences included workshops and vendor exhibits so it enabled me to be up to date on equipment, techniques, and technology as well as see how other people were handling some of the same problems I was confronting. The ability to travel and see how other people who were doing the same kind of work I was doing was helpful and interesting. It was somewhat reassuring to find that my problems weren't unique.

The Loma Prieta earthquake occurred in 1989 during my tenure as commander of the Communications Division. It occurred just after 5:00 p.m. in the evening. I was in the division at the time. My normal work hours were 7:00 a.m. to 3:00 p.m. but I was almost never able to go home on time and this date was no exception. The earthquake was 6.9 on the Richter Scale (some reports claim 7.1), and centered near Santa Cruz, California. However, it did extensive damage throughout the Bay Area. In addition to property damage, the earthquake resulted in 63 deaths with hundreds more injuries. The majority of the deaths occurred in Oakland with the collapse of the double-decked Cypress section of the Nimitz Freeway. The quake also collapsed a section of the Bay Bridge taking highway 80 from Oakland to San Francisco.

The Communications Division was on the 7th floor of the Police Administration Building (PAB) at the time of the quake. We were used to the occasional bump and rattle from the small earthquakes felt in the Bay Area, but it was soon evident that this was different. It was more severe and kept going for a long time. The quake only lasted something like 20 seconds. That's a long time when things are falling down around you and you are hearing the loud noise associated with the movement of the building and its contents.

The Communications Division didn't suffer any structural damage during the quake and all radio and telephone systems continued to function. (Thank Heavens) However, the division's 40-channel recorder took a nosedive and was destroyed. This recorder recorded all telephone lines and radio channels used by the Division, so we lost a lot of important recorded information as a result of the earthquake. In one sense it was helpful. The media immediately requested copies of radio and phone conversations around the quake, and this would have taken a lot of staff time to provide. Because of the destruction of the voice recorder, we were spared this time-consuming task. I did recover the recordings just as the quake started and several complaint operators were on the phone with citizens at the time. When the earthquake was felt initially, both the dispatcher and caller would say, "Earthquake!" Some dispatchers would attempt to calm the citizen caller but as the quake continued in magnitude and duration, almost every dispatcher said, "Holy (expletive)" just before the recording stopped as the recorder hit the floor.

The recovery from the Loma Prieta earthquake tied up police operations for several weeks as bodies were recovered from crushed cars beneath the collapsed freeway. During this time, the President of the United States, the California Governor and an assortment of politicians and bureaucrats visited the Cypress scene in Oakland. It was a major and tragic event.

Within a couple of weeks after the earthquake, I had a new multi-channel recorder installed and operational. The recorder that was destroyed in the quake was supposed to be replaced as it was old and limited in capacity. I had put a new recorder in the budget and requested the city Purchasing Department to acquire it six months earlier. As a result of the earthquake, the normal purchasing bureaucracy was suspended, and I had the new recorder up and running in a couple of weeks. That told me something about the Purchasing Department bureaucracy that I already suspected. It takes an earthquake to get anything through purchasing expeditiously.

The second major city-wide event during my time in the Communications Division was the Oakland Hills Firestorm in 1991. The fire started on a windy October day in the Oakland hills from a previous grass fire that was thought to be completely extinguished. The warm strong October wind fanned smoldering debris into a raging fire that consumed some 3000 structures and killed 25 people. The warm dry condition and strong wind blew the fire beyond the ability of the fire department, even with mutual aid, to control or contain. One of the fire fatalities was an Oakland Police officer who, after assisting citizens evacuate from a hazardous location, was overcome by a sudden flashover that prevented his escape. The heat of the fire melted the aluminum components of his police car.

The fire occurred on my day off and I happened to be in Oakland at a car dealership when I noticed an Oakland motorcycle officer responding toward the Oakland hills with red light and siren. I looked up the street in the direction he was headed and saw a huge plume of smoke in the air. Knowing that with the strong wind blowing a fire would be a serious situation, I responded to the Communications Division and remained there till well after midnight. We called in a number of off duty dispatch personnel to handle telephones and radio channels. It was a difficult day for Oakland.

In the aftermath of the fire one of the dispatchers was sued by a grieving family that lost their daughter in the fire. The girl had called 911 because she was in her house and afraid because of the smoke and fire in the area. The dispatcher told her to stay there, and he would try to get an officer to her to take her out of the area. As it turned out it was not possible to get an officer to her because of the fire and she perished. There's no protocol to tell dispatchers what to do in every situation so he used his best judgement. With a fixed location we would know where to send help. Otherwise, he could have just told her to run for it, but the fire spread so rapidly there's no knowing if she would have made it on foot. It was just a sad situation and a grieving family was seeking to fix blame on a dispatcher. The dispatcher was not harmed in court, but it took a toll on him.

I was particularly aware of how uncomfortable it is to be sued as I had been sued by a dispatcher I had terminated for cause. The dispatcher had been disciplined previously for various violations when terminated. However, the dispatcher claimed she was terminated because of racial prejudice. The dispatcher was white, but she was married to a black officer and claimed she was being disciplined because her husband was black. Of course, there was no correlation between who she was married to and the cause for which she was terminated but it was professionally embarrassing to be accused of discrimination on the basis of race in a racially sensitive city and job. In the process of giving depositions, it was demonstrated that there was cause for termination and no basis for the claim of racial discrimination and the case was dismissed with prejudice. The victory felt good, but I felt damaged by the accusation of racial discrimination.

I requested to be transferred from Communications to Patrol Division because I preferred working in Patrol to being a desk jockey. As division commander In Communications, I wore a suit and tie and worked days with Saturday and Sunday off but I felt more like a bureaucrat than a cop. I was eventually transferred to Patrol where I worked as a sector commander under a captain. Again, word may have gotten out that I was enjoying my assignment as some months down the road I was transferred back to the Communications Division where some major projects were looming on the horizon.

Upon returning to the Communications Division, I undertook some challenging projects involving a move of the facility and the implementation of new communications systems. These projects were challenging in both positive and negative ways. Positive in that they were interesting and provided a positive benefit for overall operations. They were negative in that they overlapped and involved complex coordination with multiple vendors and individuals. On top of this was the ever-present knowledge that any problems in the implementation of the new systems could be catastrophic and I would get my name in the papers in a most unpleasant context. The Communications Division must be operational for emergency and non-emergency service 24-7 as the public and field personnel require and deserve. System failure was not an option.

One of the major projects was the implementation of a new Computer Assisted Dispatch (CAD) system. The old CAD system was functional, but the supporting hardware was aged and failing. Occasional hardware failures were chaotic. In addition, we needed a new CAD system that could incorporate new features while integrating with a departmental information management system. Both new hardware and new software were required.

The police department hired its own computer programmers, and the software was developed in-house in the Planning and Research Division where I had worked many years before. A great deal of coordination and testing was required as the software was developed. New, state of the art, computer hardware was also required to handle the increased demands of the CAD system. Because of the need for durability and viability of the system under adverse conditions, the system was redundant, and we added an Uninterruptible Power System (UPS). The UPS filters all power going to the computer system to eliminate spikes that might harm the computer and provides battery backup in the event of a power failure. For long term power outages, and to keep lights and other critical systems operational, the department had a large diesel generator in the basement.

The new CAD system with UPS and associated computer equipment would be installed in the recently vacated 9th floor of the Police Administration Building. This meant the entire Communications Division would be moved from the 7th to the 9th floor. This would be no big deal for anything other than in an emergency service that must be available and operational 24-hours-a-day, seven-days-a-week. In addition to this, the move would include the installation of a new city owned telephone system and a new Automatic Call Distributing System (ACDS). The ACDS received incoming calls for service from the public, including 911 and seven-digit emergency and non-emergency lines, and connected them with complaint operators who were plugged into the system at their workstations. The ACDS also provided management information regarding calls received by line, hour of day and day of week.

All dispatch personnel had to be trained in advance on the new CAD and phone systems and the move had to be made while maintaining full emergency operations. I worked out a step-by-step process by which staff could migrate to the new facility with phone company technicians rerouting phone lines from the seventh to the ninth floor by increments.

Another major project coming to resolution at the same time as the implementation of the new CAD and telephone systems and the move to the 9th floor involved a new radio system. The new radio system involved transitioning the entire police and fire departments from a conventional radio system with dedicated radio channels to a trunked radio system which is a digitally driven system with radio channels in a pool and assigned by the system as needed with each-push-to talk.

In a conventional radio system, you select a dedicated radio channel to talk to others on that channel. With a trunked radio system, you select a digital entity known as a talk group rather than a dedicated radio channel. To talk with everyone selected on that talk group you select that talk group on your radio, just like you would select a channel but when you press the push to talk the radio system recognizes your radio and the talk group you are selected on then assigns an available radio channel from a pool of channels and switches everyone else selected on that talk group to that channel so you can communicate with them. This all happens in a split second, so it appears to operate like a conventional radio system.

If you don't have the foggiest idea about what I just described, don't worry about it. Suffice it to say that a trunked radio system is highly technical but highly efficient. In a command staff meeting the topic of the new trunked radio system came up and the chief of police asked me to describe the system to the assembled command staff. I was about a minute into the description when I noticed that virtually everyone's eyes had glazed over. I quickly learned that there's no quick way to describe how a trunked radio system works. You could just say it's a digitally switched radio system, but that definition is inadequate for someone whose life depends on how it works and how well it works. Like me at first, police personnel weren't sure they wanted to depend on a complicated computerized radio system to be there for them when having a bad day on the job.

It takes time to give an adequate description of a trunked radio system with all its features and benefits. I loved the technology and enjoyed describing the trunked radio system to fellow officers while watching their glazed eyes of skepticism turn into nodding heads of understanding with reduced skepticism. Even after understanding the technology, I had to see it in operation to fully appreciate and trust trunked radio technology.

The acquisition of the trunked radio system went through the normal, bureaucratic purchasing process and Ericsson-GE and Motorola were the only two bidders. The Ericsson-GE bid was clearly more responsive to our specifications, but Motorola objected to certain City Council members and there were meetings involving a mix of technology and politics. Fortunately, city communications engineers were the big hitters, and they were in my camp.

In the final stages of vendor selection, we met with Ericsson-GE people at their manufacturing facility in Lynchburg Virginia and visited a law enforcement agency in Florida using the Ericsson-GE trunked radio system. I was confident in the technology after meeting with Florida law enforcement users and seeing the system in operation.

I ended up training trainers from the various divisions of the Oakland Police Department how to train others in their respective divisions on the pending trunked radio system. To minimize glazed eyes, I created a training manual that included pictures and diagrams. We also had to train the Police Communications Dispatcher staff on the new radio system.

I arranged for the move of the Communications Division and implementation of the new CAD, phone and radio systems to take place at 3:00 a.m. during the slowest time of the day. By 6:00 a.m. we were relocated, and everything was running reasonably well. A casual observer from the outside would have seen the transition like a duck moving peacefully across a pond. What they didn't see was that under the water or behind the scenes and out of sight, the duck's legs were paddling furiously to move it forward. Much to my surprise, while I felt some exhilaration in the success of the operation, a feeling of depression was overtaking me. A number of people from around the department came by to congratulate me but I just wanted to be alone. After months of planning and stressful preparation we had successfully transitioned to new equipment in a new facility without getting my name in the papers. I decided my depression must be something like postpartum depression. Months of work, stress and anticipation had come to an abrupt end. The depression went away in a few days and I was ready for what came next.

Of course, there were some problems with each system and transition pains here and there but all and all it went well without a major disaster. There were the usual happy and unhappy campers to deal with, but most issues were minor. Most importantly, the transition had been accomplished without compromising public safety.

In the months that followed the completion of the major projects I again requested to be transferred back to the Patrol Division. I was nearing the end of my OPD career and I wanted to leave from Patrol. There was a small financial benefit if I retired from Patrol and I wanted one last taste of the street.

Eventually my request was granted, and I was transferred to Patrol Division. With my seniority, I ended up on day watch with another lieutenant but no captain. Normally a watch was staffed by a captain and two lieutenants. Each lieutenant took command of half the city, the east or west sector. With no captain on our watch, I would be acting captain when the other lieutenant was off, and he would be acting captain when I was on days off. On days we both worked we took turns on which one of us would be acting captain and get the additional acting pay. This arrangement was less than desirable as we were reluctant to take any days off apart from our regular days off because it required the other lieutenant to be there, even if on his scheduled days off.

The arrangement was also unfortunate because without a captain the other lieutenant and I ended up with a lot of extra paperwork and bureaucratic duties. I had a hard time getting out of the office and on the street unless there was some sort of major incident.

After a few months, a captain was assigned to the watch, but he didn't appear to absorb much of the paperwork and I still had a hard time getting out of the office. I had never really aspired to the rank of Captain of Police as most of the assignments were management or bureaucratic, except for the captains in Patrol Division where there was opportunity to get out of the office and onto the street. I had experienced all the bureaucratic and management assignments I cared for, so I was not highly motivated for the rank. I did take the captain's promotion exam once but was too low on the list to be appointed. I had done very little preparation and study for the exam, so it wasn't much of a disappointment.

After a few months saying goodbye to Patrol, I was ready to say goodbye to the Oakland Police Department. All in all, I could say that it was a good career involving a wide variety of assignments. I had come to know and appreciate many fellow officers, police dispatchers and civilian personnel. I was proud to have been an Oakland Police Officer, but city politics were changing, and I was ready to move on. On July 7th, 1995, I retired from the Oakland Police Department.

During my 28 and a half years on OPD, 14 officer had been killed. This included one in the Oakland Hills Firestorm and two in a helicopter crash. The rest were shot in the line of duty. Many more were shot or injured in other ways but survived.

I characterize my retirement from OPD as bitter-sweet. It was slightly bitter as I was leaving respected friends and a familiar organization behind me. But it was sweet in that I was moving on to a new job opportunity. I had been in touch with a former sergeant who worked for me in the Communications Division. He had retired from OPD and joined the Bay

Area Rapid Transit (BART) police department, and he was enjoying the work with BART PD. On a day off at OPD, I spent a day working with the retired sergeant who was now a BART officer. It was an interesting day working out of Powell Street BART station in San Francisco and I decided to apply to BART PD.

CHAPTER 11

BART POLICE DEPARTMENT

I applied for the position of Police Officer with the Bay Area Rapid Transit (BART) District knowing I would be leaving the rank of lieutenant in one agency to become an entry level officer in another agency. This greatly appealed to me. I was tired of being a bureaucrat and supervisor and I was ready to just be in charge of myself doing a job that had appealed to me so many years before. I was looking forward to a change and something new while I still had some energy left and was willing to put myself into the blue.

While I had been a police officer for many years, I had to go through the BART PD selection process just like everyone else. I passed the written exam, oral interview, physical agility test, written and oral psychiatric evaluation and a background investigation. In the physical agility test I had pulled a muscle in my back early in the testing but managed to mask the pain and complete the rest of the testing.

On June 22nd, while still working at OPD, I received a phone call from BART advising that my first day of work with BART PD would be July 17th, 1995. With this information, I drafted my letter of retirement from OPD to be effective July 7th.

I was one of four new officers reporting to BART PD on July 17th. All of us were transitioning from another police agency. One other was from OPD, one was from the University of California Police Department at Berkeley and one had been a School Security Officer with Oakland Public Schools. We were sworn in by the BART PD chief and I received my BART PD badge #363. We were issued equipment and a few pounds worth of manuals and another pound of keys to various facilities around the BART system. We were assigned lockers in the Lake Merritt BART Station in downtown Oakland.

In addition to firearms training with newly issued weapons, we spent about a week and a half on an orientation tour of the BART system with stations throughout the San Francisco Bay Area. We were made aware of each BART station and the best routes between stations when on vehicle patrol. We were in parts of the Bay Area that were quite unfamiliar to me.

After the orientation we were assigned to work regular shifts with officers who were designated Field Training Officers (FTOs). We were probationary officers for six months during our training and during this time we were given periodic written tests on BART and BART PD rules and regulations. I passed a final exam in November. During our probationary period we were assigned to work with FTOs at various locations around the system. I worked out of stations from San Francisco to Richmond, to Oakland, to Concord to Hayward to Fremont. All this moving around was helpful to become familiar with the BART system and to work with various officers with their various styles, interests, and areas of expertise.

In early December, I was off probation and training status and assigned as a solo officer working out of the Hayward BART station. It was interesting to note that while at OPD we had a formal lineup often with inspections before going on the street, there was nothing like this with BART PD. With officers reporting at different locations throughout the system there may or may not be a sergeant to greet you, let alone hold a formal lineup. You were expected to be on duty, in uniform and ready to work at the appointed time and location.

One of the things I enjoyed about working as a BART police officer was the chance to interface with the public in something other than a crisis situation. Working as a beat officer in Oakland you spent much of your time going from crime to crisis. The pace at BART was much slower.

We had two kinds of beat assignments at BART; you could be assigned as a patrol car officer or a train officer. Either way, you were assigned to patrol a range of the system that normally included up to four stations. If you were on a train beat you would ride the trains between your assigned stations walking through the cars to see and be seen. You would also walk through the various stations on your beat to see and be seen. Officers on vehicle patrol would patrol the parking lots and parking structures as well as the system trackways and stations on your beat.

BART Police handle most of the same types of calls for service that are handled by municipal police departments but much of the routine work was related to BART operations. Eating and drinking were prohibited on the trains and we enforced those rules. Street people ne'er-do-wells were constantly trying to sneak onto BART trains to travel for free. These were called fare evaders and catching fare evaders was something like a sport. Early on I learned how to hide behind walls and peek through cracks to catch fare evaders. Initially I was embarrassed by this technique. Wasn't I supposed to be catching bank robbers? Here I was sneaking and peeking to catch someone sneaking in or out of BART. Yes, you can sneak out as well as into BART.

The way the BART system works, the rider first purchases a ticket from a vending machine. They then insert the ticket into a fare gate that reads and returns the ticket and opens the fare gate to let the ticketed person enter the BART system. The fare gate closes behind the ticketed person and the next person has to use their own ticket to enter BART. Once inside the BART system, the person with the ticket can ride anywhere they want. However, to exit the system they must insert their ticket into the exit gate which reads the ticket, subtracts the fare charge based on where they entered the system, and returns the ticket while opening the gate for the ticketed person to leave the system. If the person doesn't have enough money on the ticket for the fare, the ticket is returned but the fare gate won't open, and they must add money to the ticket in order to exit the system. Usually there's a small booth near the entrance and exit gates staffed by a Station Agent who can assist people with problems they may encounter.

What makes catching fare evaders a sport is the challenge to catch them in the act. I likened it to fishing on the ranch where I grew up.

Every once in a while, you catch a big one, like a fare evader with a felony warrant. Catching fare evaders was part of the job so peeking from behind walls soon moved from embarrassment to anticipation.

Of course the fare evader that jumps over the waist high fence that separates the free part of the station from the paid area of the system was easy picking. It was a little more difficult to catch a piggy backer. The piggy backer walks close behind a person with a valid ticket and pretends to insert a ticket into the fare gate but actually slips into or out of the system before the gate closes behind the ticketed party. You have to watch close to catch this fish.

The first fare evasion ticket I wrote was in Civic Center station in San Francisco. A street person pushed open a gate and walked out of the paid area of the system into the free area without using a ticket to exit. He did this right in front of me but didn't see me until I stopped him and asked to see his ticket. He had to have a ticket to enter the system so if he exited without using or having a ticket, he was a fare evader. He didn't have a ticket so I gave him one. We usually just issued a citation to fare evaders. It would only result in an arrest if there were warrants or other charges.

I soon found that many people, especially street people, routinely evade fares and get citations which they don't pay, and which go into a warrant for failure to appear. When I wrote someone a citation for fare evasion it was common to find they had a number of warrants for previous citations and failures to appear. Once the warrants got into the thousands of dollars it was worth our time to arrest them. They would go to jail then to court in a day or so where all warrants were forgiven for "time served" and we would start the process over with the next citation. It was a game for them and a sport for me. I did my thing; they did their thing, and the world kept turning.

There were other types of fare evaders to look for. Certain tickets are discounted. All tickets are color-coded by type of ticket. If an adult uses a colored ticket that was discounted for juveniles, you could cite them for fare evasion. In San Francisco the BART stations along Market Street are deep underground and the San Francisco Muni rail system runs above the BART system. Using television monitors in the Station Agent's booth, we could see someone enter the elevator on the BART level and get off the elevator at the Muni level where they would go up the stairs and walk out into the free area of the station with the Muni riders who don't have to pay a fare to exit. This is just another way the game was played.

Not everyone who knows the BART to Muni free exit plan was a street person. I cited one young lady for that violation who insisted that she didn't know it was a violation. She also played games with her name and identification, so I detained her until I knew who she was and, in the process determined she had prior violations. Some weeks later she stopped me in the Powell Street station to inform me she told the court that she didn't know it was a violation, so the charge was dismissed without a fine. This didn't bother me as I was familiar with the "justice" system and I was pretty sure she wouldn't do it again. My mission was accomplished.

In addition to catching fare evaders as a BART officer, I made arrests for possession of drugs, disturbing the peace, indecent exposure, battery and took reports on robbery and auto theft...the usual stuff an officer in a municipal area might encounter. We also dealt with what we called lodgers. They were usually street people who would sneak into areas of the system not open to the public or after hours of operation in order to find an indoor warm place to sleep. Pan handlers were a problem in many areas of the system. Most of the crimes or infractions were minor but had to be enforced to make the system safe and comfortable for the public.

My favorite assignments while working BART was when I was working train beats. I enjoyed riding and walking through trains while traveling between stations. It gave the public a sense of police presence and safety and I liked being on my feet rather than in a police car. Toward the end of a shift, I could get pretty tired as officers were not allowed to sit down while riding trains. We worked 10-hour shifts and got three-day weekends which I loved. However, the 10-hour shifts on your feet could be tiresome. Still, I found I could stumble into some good cases while walking trains. In addition to fare evaders and lodgers, I once came upon a young man packaging his weed on his BART seat. On another occasion, a lady grabbed me as I walked by because a young man had been exposing himself to her. You never know what trouble you can find if you're really looking for it.

Street people would sneak onto trains to sleep in a warm place during the day. I once found what appeared to be and smelled like a street person sleeping across two seats on a crowded train heading toward Walnut Creek from the Lafayette station. I woke him up and told him to sit up and not to take up more than one seat. I asked him where he was going. He said Powell Street. That's in San Francisco so I told him it was over 24,000 miles in the direction he was headed and a lot shorter if he was on a train going the other direction. I asked to see his ticket upon which he ritually felt all his pockets and, without checking inside any pocket told me he didn't have one. I put him off the train and gave him a ticket in the form of a citation. This is typical activity when on a train beat.

I was outrun by fare evaders on more than one occasion but all the gear I was wearing, and the age difference gave them the advantage. Running an offender off is not as satisfying as writing them a ticket but the message is still delivered. For me it was a sport, but not a running sport.

One rainy day a fare evader split from me at the Coliseum BART station in Oakland before I could write him a ticket. When I first detained him I used my radio to contact dispatch to see if he had any outstanding warrants before I cited him. I was informed he had a minor warrant and he apparently heard this and took off running. I pursued him a short distance and saw him cut across a drainage area with water up to his waist as he fled into a nearby housing project. I wasn't about to follow a fare evader through a swamp into the projects, so I advised dispatch that my disposition was R&R which stood for Reprimand and Release. In this case however, it also stood for Ran like a Rabbit.

The BART system was plagued by street people who find clever ways to swindle the public out of their money. I took a report from a couple of young UC Berkeley college students on a BART train platform who were swindled out of some significant money by a guy playing a shell game using bottle caps and a tinfoil ball. His overhead was minimal, but he invested in the ignorance of a couple of youngsters who thought they could beat him at his game. The swindler was nowhere in sight when I arrived, but the students got an advanced degree in street smarts.

I just missed a swindler when working a train beat at the Union City BART station. The victim had not used BART before, and the swindler spotted her standing in front of a BART ticket machine trying to figure out how to buy a ticket. The swindler offered to help her buy a ticket and she gladly accepted his "assistance." He showed her how much her ticket would cost based on where she was going and encouraged her to buy a round trip ticket so she could return to the Union City station. He showed her where to insert her money and told her would get her ticket for her by pushing the buttons for her. He had pushed the coin return button and reached where the ticket would be dispensed and palmed a used ticket he had found in a garbage can. He gave her the used ticket and pointed her to the fare gate where she would enter BART with her ticket. When she turned to head for the fare gates the swindler took all her money from the coin return and split. When the used ticket wouldn't open the fare gate for her, the station agent checked the ticket and determined it was used and had no money left on it. That's when I arrived but the swindler was long gone.

All law enforcement work has an element of hazard to it but I enjoyed my time as a train or beat officer with BART. Compared to Oakland, it was police work lite. I usually had time to talk with people who weren't criminal suspects or victims of crimes. Over time I learned where the Starbucks were located relative to the various stations and beats and I would usually have time to enjoy a cup of coffee during my shift. It wasn't unusual to only have one or two dispatched calls for service to handle during an 8-hour shift.

While BART was policework lite compared to my time on Oakland, I ended up with my worst on duty injury while working for BART. One swing shift another officer and I were dispatched to intercept a train coming into the Richmond BART station with a man causing a disturbance on board. As we boarded the train, passengers pointed out a drunk ex-con who had been creating a disturbance. We took him off the train and handcuffed him with his hands behind his back. I stayed with him while the other officer went back into the train to see if there was an offense other than drunk and disorderly.

To minimize the drunk's mobility, I faced him against a waist-high barrier wall around the escalator opening where there were up and down escalators between the train platform where we were and the street level down below. I stood behind and held the drunk ex-con's arm to further minimize his mobility. However, he pushed back and threw one of his legs over the barrier and tried to lean forward as if to get away over the barrier. There was a long drop to the floor below if he were to go over the barrier and with arms handcuffed behind him it would be a fatal fall, so I pulled him backward to try to get him to remove his leg from over the barrier. For several seconds I would pull him back and he would lunge forward.

Then, on one occasion when I was trying to pull him back, he put his foot on the barrier and pushed back as I pulled. With this sudden shift of weight, I was going over backward but tried to take some of his weight so he wouldn't hit his head on the cement platform. I don't know exactly what position my leg was in but as we went down, I felt my ankle break, it felt like an electric shock. I held my prisoner down as my partner arrived. I told her I thought my leg was broken. She called for another officer and an ambulance. I was stupid and canceled the ambulance. I didn't want to be hauled off in an ambulance if it turned out my ankle was only sprained and not broken. I managed to walk slowly and painfully to my car and drive myself to the hospital where it was determined that the ankle was broken. I had never broken a bone before, and I don't think I did myself any favors by walking on the broken ankle.

The broken ankle was repaired by what they called an open reduction, internal fixation surgery. That turned out of be a surgery where they put the bones back together and use screws and a metal plate to secure the broken parts together. It was a long recovery as it was slowed by infection and took a lot of physical therapy to get everything working right again. At one point the doctor told me I might not be able to return to work if it didn't heal well. This upset me as I knew the BART Police Department was counting on me to be involved when BART transitioned from a conventional radio system to a trunked radio system. With my trunked radio background with the Oakland Police Department, I knew I could be of assistance with BART's pending transition from a conventional to a trunked radio system.

Fortunately, with the physical therapy I was able to return to work for BART PD. I have a metal plate in my ankle and there's a slight limitation in ankle flexibility, but it has not proven to be much of a problem. I was pleased to work out of the BART police substation at the San Francisco Powell Street BART station for several months before being called on to work on the BART transition to a trunked radio system.

I was not involved in the acquisition of BART's trunked radio system - those decisions had been made and I was coming in as BART was preparing to acquire and implement the system. I was quite happy with this since I was going to work with a trunked radio system implementation. I would be working with all of the technology I loved, but I was not in charge.

Everything could crash and burn, and I wouldn't get my name in the papers. I could just walk away and say, "Boy, that was a mess" and nothing would stick to me.

For a time, I worked on things related to the coming trunked radio system and on various police department assignments. I was pleased to find that Ericsson G.E. was to be BART's trunked system provider as I had worked with them at Oakland. I was working with a familiar system and with familiar people. Ericsson G.E. referred to their trunked system as EDACS which stood for Enhanced Digital Access Communications System. I attended EDACS user group conferences in New Orleans and Niagara Falls, Canada, and we toured a working EDACS system in Los Angeles. Eventually, I was loaned from the police department to a BART engineering group that was tasked with the responsibility of implementing the trunked radio system throughout the BART system. I shared an office with the group in downtown Oakland. Not only would the BART Police Department be using the system but everyone from train operators to station agents to maintenance personnel would be using the trunked radio system. My primary responsibility was to facilitate the police department's transition to the system, but I interfaced with other system users. I also coordinated with the Oakland Police Department and the Richmond Police Department who also were using EDACS systems. I wanted to ensure that the BART police had common talk groups (think something like a radio channel) on which we could communicate for mutual aid situations.

I worked on radio programs for various user groups within the BART system with an emphasis on radio programs for the BART Police Department. As I described how the trunked system worked to BART users in and out of the police department, I saw the same blank looks, glazed eyes of doubt and fielded the same questions I encountered when trunked radio was introduced at the Oakland Police Department. I ended up training BART Police Department personnel on the new system. I provided handouts and gave demonstrations as part of the training which took several days. I almost lost my voice in the process of the training but managed to get through it. I was also tasked with drafting orders and procedures to follow when using the trunked radio system and what to do in the event of system failure.

BART's transition from conventional to the trunked system took place at 2:00 a.m. on a Sunday morning. Just like at Oakland, we wanted to make the transition at a time when activity was at its lowest. The transition went reasonably well with minor transitional issues one might expect. All the right equipment was available and in place at the right time and locations throughout the system.

The major part of the radio system transition was behind me. While there were meetings with various user groups and time spent on equipment and operational issues, my role in the transition was coming to an end. I decided that, rather than go back to the street as a working officer, the job was best left to younger officers. I was not as physically strong as I felt I should be on the job. My ankle break had healed but it was a point of vulnerability and occasional pain. I had contributed what I could to BART Police Department, and I retired on October 20th, 2000.

CHAPTER 12

IN CONCLUSION

At the end of a 34-year career in law enforcement I sometimes look back and wonder if I made a difference. I can't say I ever saved a life or made anyone's life better, but I am confident I was doing something important and something I believed in. I was just a cog in an imperfect and cumbersome wheel of justice but it's the cogs that make it work. I had entered a career in law enforcement as a naïve idealist with ideas about justice and being the good guy standing between crime and an appreciative public. I had survived the realities of the street and the criminal justice system without becoming a bitter cynic. I had discovered that the public was not always appreciative of law enforcement. After all, I can understand how it's difficult to appreciate your local law enforcement while they are writing you a traffic citation. For some I was the problem, not the solution. For others with criminal intentions, I was the enemy. I found that a portion of the population would dislike me because I was white and/or because I was a police officer. Of course, if I were a black, Asian or Hispanic police officer, some people would dislike me for that. Mankind is one race but fallen and prone to make unwarranted distinctions and generalizations. Some disliked me because they disliked the laws I enforced, or I represented an authority or system they disliked.

In a sense, law enforcement is a career on the edge of civilization. We are something like a wedge driven between social order and chaos. We work in that often-hazy place between right and wrong, good and bad, justice and injustice. These concepts seem clear in the abstract, but they become hazy in the application within a changing social and political matrix with conflicting and evolving societal standards. As social priorities and values change, society's laws often come into conflict. Laws don't always reflect society's current actual values, yet they represent standards or ideals that a large portion of society cannot reject. Many people think that police shouldn't be enforcing certain petty or victimless crimes but at the same time don't want to live in neighborhoods filled with drug users, prostitutes, panhandlers and petty crime. That leaves law enforcement in an awkward position when we enforce laws that are not universally appreciated. In a strange sense, we are paid to bite the hand that feeds us. We are the help that takes care of society's dirty linen. We go to places and do things that "good" people shouldn't have to deal with. If the linen is dirty, we are called upon to clean it up or we can be blamed for it – sometimes rightly so.

Was I still an idealist after some 34 years in law enforcement? I think so, but for certain, I was not the naïve idealist who entered law enforcement. There are moments when I miss the naivety I started with, but it has been replaced with experience and reality. All in all, it was a good career where I had the opportunity to be a street cop, a supervisor, a manager, a bureaucrat, and a technical worker. I took some lumps, but I had served my country, I was paid well and worked with and for some fine people. I managed to dissipate the inevitable cynicism that comes with the job through humor. I was an idealist that hit the wall of reality without becoming a cynic. That said, occasional cynicism is not a stranger to me.

I continue to believe in the role of law enforcement in our culture and this great country. However, I now understand more fully that those of us in law enforcement are fallible, fallen people serving fallible, fallen people in a fallible, fallen system. We are a necessary force or agency in any culture. In the short run, law enforcement is a worthy goal but justice will sometimes slip through cracks in the system. I had to learn not to worry too much about this because I could be confident that, in the long run justice is absolute as every knee will bow before its creator. So, in the end, I'm still an idealist, but an informed idealist.

I think law enforcement would do well to attract idealists rather than just somebody looking for a job. An idealist will be self-motivated because they believe in their job and want to make a positive difference. The idealists will have to temper their idealism with the hard realities of the street and an imperfect justice system, but if they can avoid debilitating cynicism, they will do well. Early in my career I heard a high-ranking command officer say essentially this same thing in a bit crude but more succinct way. His advice was, "Don't let the bastards drag you down." That is still good advice for an idealist aspiring to wear the blue.

I encourage the reader to give a smile and a friendly nod the next time you see a man or woman wearing the blue or whatever color of uniform they might wear. They are just like you doing a sometimes-difficult job. If you feel inclined, say, "thank you" it's always good to hear and they may not have heard it in a while. Of course, if they are writing you a ticket, the "thank you" is optional.